AF725507

Pankaj Madan attended Leeds Grammar School and then Magdalene College, Cambridge where he read Law. He was called to the Bar in 1997. He undertook pupillage in Leeds. He is a practising Barrister and full tenant at both 12 King's Bench Walk, London (since 2008) and Exchange Chambers, Leeds, Manchester and Liverpool (since 2012).

Pankaj grew up within a medical family and is recommended by the Legal 500 for "his superb strategic approach to brain injury cases" and "a brilliant client manner". He is praised for his "wealth of experience in subtle and catastrophic brain injury claims".

He represents both Claimants and Defendants usually only in high value severe, life-changing or catastrophic injury cases. The latter usually involve brain injury claims.

He has an excellent understanding of medical issues. He is a member of the Royal Society of Medicine Pain Section Council, the first lawyer ever to be invited to sit, and has addressed two international conferences held at the Royal Society of Medicine.

Pankaj is routinely instructed nationally by leading firms. He is sought after by insurers and defence firms too and adopts a team approach with the insurer and Solicitor. He has been a Deputy District Judge for over 13 years and has considerable expertise in costs management of high value cases for both Claimants and Defendants.

He is experienced in claims of the utmost severity exceeding £20 million.

Pankaj enjoys keeping fit, trail and fell-running, travel, the theatre and the opera and ballet.

He is from a medical family background and is married to a Consultant Child Psychiatrist and is a dad.

A Practical Guide to Catastrophic Brain Injury Claims

A Practical Guide to Catastrophic Brain Injury Claims

Pankaj Madan
Barrister,
Exchange Chambers, Leeds, Manchester, Liverpool
& 12 King's Bench Walk, Temple, London

Law Brief Publishing

© Pankaj Madan

All rights reserved. No part of this publication may be reproduced, stored in a retrieval system, or transmitted, in any form or by any means, electronic, mechanical, photocopying, recording or otherwise, without the prior permission of the publisher.

Excerpts from judgments and statutes are Crown copyright. Any Crown Copyright material is reproduced with the permission of the Controller of OPSI and the King's Printer for Scotland. Some quotations may be licensed under the terms of the Open Government Licence (http://www.nationalarchives.gov.uk/doc/open-government-licence/version/3).

Cover image © iStockphoto.com/bekisha

The information in this book was believed to be correct at the time of writing. All content is for information purposes only and is not intended as legal advice. No liability is accepted by either the publisher or author for any errors or omissions (whether negligent or not) that it may contain. Professional advice should always be obtained before applying any information to particular circumstances.

Published 2024 by Law Brief Publishing, an imprint of Law Brief Publishing Ltd
30 The Parks
Minehead
Somerset
TA24 8BT

www.lawbriefpublishing.com

Paperback: 978-1-912687-01-5

PREFACE

"You do Catastrophic Brain Injury too don't you?" said my instructing solicitor to be. He'd just bought and read my first book "A Practical Guide to Subtle Brain Injury" and wanted to be sure. "Yes, I said". "Well, I've got one for you" I don't think you'll take it mind. Looks like he just walked in front of a car". "I'll send you the papers though". "Thanks" I said.

"How do you know?" I said.

"know what" he said.

"That he just walked in front of a car?" I asked.

"Oh… there's some CCTV". "Haven't watched it yet mind, just going off what the witnesses say".

"Okay, perhaps you can send the CCTV to me I said".

I played the CCTV straight away. I watched in horror as the "Smart" car drove straight into my unfortunate stationary client standing in the middle of the road. "Hmm. Smart car, dumb driver I thought". The Claimant was waiting for traffic to clear but was looking one way not both ways. The car coming from his right drove into him and didn't brake until after hitting him.

To cut a long story short, (and that's sort of the point of this book), 3 years later the case settled for over £5 million and was approved in the High Court. Four points here:-

1. Don't take anybody's word for it. Particularly in this area, and with the potential values. Dot every "I" and cross every "T" yourself.

2. Make your own mind up. Make no assumptions. Be determined.

3. I was reminded of the value of timeously preserving the evidence. This and some excellent reconstruction evidence ensured it was a sure-fire winning case.

4. The case demonstrated the effect of average as opposed to excellent rehabilitation. Despite the CCTV evidence and reconstruction, the Defendant sadly wouldn't offer a penny by way of interim payments, maintaining to the end that they "would win" when they would not. It may have cost them more in the end, who knows, but it certainly made life much worse for a catastrophically injured Claimant and his family. Excellent rehabilitation makes a difference most of the time.

I felt that it would be useful to produce a guide, another "small"? practical book specifically on Catastrophic Brain Injury with handy checklists and reminders that you can take around with you. Pilots don't go into a cockpit without checklists. Why should it be different for catastrophic brain injury lawyers?

Catastrophic brain injury is usually very obvious. Whilst subtle traumatic brain injury may in its own way have temporary or permanent effects and be very serious it is not as obvious.

With catastrophic brain injury there will have always been marked prolonged loss of consciousness, sometimes for many months. In Subtle Brain Injury claims, the issue is usually whether the Claimant has suffered an organic injury or not.

In Catastrophic Injury claims the disputes centre around what will the Claimant require and for how long he, she or they will require it. Life expectancy issues are often in dispute here and the extent and nature of the care package.

In the worst cases, consciousness may never be regained. There will be marked permanent changes often motor, speech, emotional and cognitive and the consequent loss of ability to lead anything approaching a remotely normal life. There will usually be a life-long need for professional care and support. There will almost inevitably be a loss of mental capacity leading to a claim for Deputyship costs. Proceedings will usually be through a Litigation Friend or the Official Solicitor.

I aim here to provide a concise guide giving practical advice and reminders to those lawyers dealing with catastrophic brain injuries.

I do so with great humility. There are Silks and Senior solicitors and Senior Junior Counsel, who may have equal or more experience than me. Nobody knows everything in this area and no one person can know everything there is to know. We can only continue learning and help to inform each other.

Also, I cannot cover everything. My aim is to provide a short guide to help those bringing and defending such claims. A reminder and easy references of the principal points for those who are more experienced, a pathfinder for those who are perhaps just setting out in this area of personal injury perhaps with their first case, finding their way, hopefully at first assisting a senior solicitor or two, of course.

Again, there is much medicine in this area of the law. I am not a doctor. I have attempted to understand this complex area from experience, medical reports, talking to medical experts, reading medical books and articles. I do not list them all here. They are too numerous. I do not mean to be controversial. I try to simplify. By necessity, this can leave out what some may consider to be important. For that I can only apologise.

As before, I want to make it clear that I have no bias towards Claimants or towards Defendants. Indeed, I act for both, although more Claimant work than Defendant has found me in recent years but through no conscious choice. As members of the Bar, in my opinion we should act for whosoever wants us.

There is every opportunity in this area of law particularly for a collaborative approach. People are mostly well-advised to adopt it.

Finally, I would like to give thanks to William Waldron K.C, Head of Exchange Chambers, a Silk of great charm, kindness, ability and humility who has led me on so many occasions now. A great mentor and friend who has taught me so much and continues to do so.

And equally to the incredibly bright and astute, William Audland KC, of 12 King's Bench Walk my Head of Chambers, who continues to be a great mentor, friend and supporter.

Finally, to my wife Monica, my parents for all they have done and continue to do.

The law is believed to be accurate at 30th April 2024.

Pankaj Madan
April 2024

CONTENTS

CHAPTER ONE

THE STRUCTURE OF THE BRAIN

Catastrophic brain injury is "double the trouble". These are difficult cases to deal with. Catastrophic brain injury often provides a similar level of *physical* difficulty as a severe spinal cord injury or amputation with the added effect of very severe *cognitive* and *emotional* impairment to add into the mix.

There will usually be dependence upon nursing support for at least one of these reasons if not all. There may be dependence on a Financial and sometimes a Welfare Deputy.

The structure of the brain

Readers of my practical guide to subtle brain injury will have to please forgive any element of repetition from the brief exposition of the structure of the brain which is set out in that book.

The brain is made up of axons which extend outward from the cell body increasing the surface area of the cell.

The axon is the elongated fibre which that extends from the cell body. It is often covered in a fatty shielding substance called myelin. Axons then connect with other cells in the body, other neurons, muscle tissue, and organs at junctions called "synapses". The chemicals which cross the synapses are called "neurotransmitters". Electrical signals as well as chemical ones called "action potentials" also communicate information or signals between cells. There are perhaps around 100 identified neurotransmitters, consisting of 6 types. One type are acetylcholines. Amino-acids are another type.

Neurons however are also different to other cells in the body. Crucially, shortly after birth, and in contrast to other types of cell, neurons in most parts of the brain stop reproducing so the adult human has a fixed number of them. The neurons within the hippocampus, a seahorse shaped structure deep within the brain (responsible for memory amongst other things) and the olfactory bulb (dealing with taste and smell) are exceptions.

Neurons are however able to form new connections with other neurons throughout life. These two facts are important to understand brain injury and rehabilitation. We cannot usually re-generate new brain cells but it is possible to find alternative and new pathways using undamaged brain cells. Neurons possess generally around 1000-10,000 connections to other neurons and 1000 "trillion" synaptic connections. A "trillion" is a million million.

Estimates of memory capacity of the human brain if one were to compare it to a computer seem to vary from around 1 Terabyte to 1000 Terabytes of data. There are 1000 Gigabytes in a Terabyte. An average computer hard drive may be around 500GB so best estimates mean that the human brain may store 2000 times the information as the average modern computer.

So, the brain, is complex. It consists of lots of neurons but also structural cells called "Glial Cells" and "Astrocytes" which support and protect the neurons. As you would expect, the brain is also very rich in a network of blood vessels to support and nourish the cells.

The brain is surrounded by the "dura" a thick protective membrane which is next to the skull. There are two further membranes, the "arachnoid" which is more loosely attached, and then the "pia mater" which is closely attached to the brain.

It is then held and protected within the skull in a cushion of fluid called the" cerebro-spinal fluid".

The skull is of course extremely hard and unyielding. One ton of pressure is needed to deform and reduce the skull diameter by 1 centimetre. This is what protects the brain from external knocks.

It is this hard unyielding cavity however which can ironically contribute to catastrophic injury to the brain. It means that the brain if injured internally through sub-dural haematoma has no space to expand. This can result in increased intra-cranial pressure which can injure the deep structures of the brain.

The brain itself can be broadly divided into 3 parts.

The 4 sections uppermost towards the skull are together called the "cerebrum". The cerebrum controls the "higher" level brain functions.

The 4 parts are called:-

1. <u>The frontal lobe</u>- the area occupying the front half of the skull;
2. <u>The parietal lobe</u>- the area immediately behind the front half of the skull on top of the head;
3. <u>The occipital lobe-</u> the area at the back of the head above the neck;
4. <u>The temporal lobe</u>- the area at the sides of the brain and extending to behind the ears.

<u>The frontal lobe</u>

The frontal lobe controls executive function, decision making skills, personality, language, planning and movement. There is a right and left frontal lobe, one in each of the hemispheres. It is the very essence of "who you are", your personality. The left frontal lobe controls language, verbal skills and positive emotions whilst the right frontal lobe tends to control non-verbal communication and negative emotions. When you are searching for the right word to say, the frontal lobe is responsible. It is also responsible for judgment and attention span regulating mood and emotions. The frontal lobe is also responsible for retaining long term memories which are not task based. Executive based tasks such as planning for the future, organisation and multi-tasking are dealt with by the frontal lobe. The frontal lobe at the point where it rests on the cribiform plate is particularly vulnerable to diffuse axonal injury. This sort of interference with higher level executive functions and personality changes are a very common complaint following trauma.

If the front part is damaged, any of the following may result:

- Difficulty processing and retaining new information
- Reduced fluency of speech
- Apathy
- Inattentiveness
- Delayed responses to questions
- A lack of inhibition, including socially inappropriate behaviour

If the middle part of the frontal lobe is damaged, people may become apathetic, inattentive and unmotivated. They may describe their thinking as "slowed".

If the middle back part of the frontal lobe is damaged people may have difficulty in expressing themselves in words (expressive aphasia)

The back part of the frontal lobe controls voluntary movement. Weakness or spasticity or paralysis can result from frontal lobe damage.

The left side of the lobe controls the right side of the body and the right side of the lobe controls the left side of the body.

The parietal lobe

The parietal lobe controls intelligence, reasoning, sensation, and our ability to read. Taste, temperature and touch are co-ordinated here. This lobe processes sensory information. Spatial sense is also co-ordinated and processed here. Knowledge of numbers and numeracy is controlled here. The ability to read, interpret words, letters and other symbols is controlled here too. The right hemisphere is more active in left hand dominant people and the left side of the lobe is more active in right hand dominant people.

Damage to the parietal lobe may cause difficulty in recognising or sensing objects by touch. It can cause numbness or impair sensation on one side of the body. People cannot sometimes tell right from left as easily and may have problems sensing where parts of their body are (proprioception).

If the right side of the parietal lobe is damaged people may be unable to do simple tasks such as brushing their hair or dressing themselves. They may have trouble drawing and may get lost in places which should be familiar to them.

The occipital lobe

The occipital lobe is largely responsible for vision. It is the main centre for the processing of visual information. If the occipital lobe is damaged on both sides of the brain people may have severely impaired vision or even go blind even though the eyes are physically working fine. This is called cortical blindness. The front part of the lobe controls recognition of familiar objects and people. In some cases vision may become partial. Blocks of visual deficit, (Hemianopia) can occur (loss of half the visual field). As well as direct injury to the back of the head, dissection of a vessel or interruption of the blood supply to this part of the brain in severe frontal or rearward collisions can result in visual deficits.

The temporal lobe

The temporal lobe is responsible for language, behaviour, hearing, vision, emotions and memory. The left side of the lobe in most people tends to control language. Damage to the left side of the lobe can therefore result in loss of memory for words and there is often impairment of the ability to understand language.

Areas of the right temporal lobe tend to control recognition of sound and music. This can result in difficulty in singing.

Damage to the temporal lobe can also result in a lack of a sense of humour, obsessiveness, hallucination of bad smells, and they may have a sense of not being able to control their feelings and a sense of "fuzzy" thinking.

Deeper structures

Beneath the cerebrum is the "cerebellum" a structure which controls balance, co-ordination and fine muscle control. Damage to this structure may result not so much from direct impact but as a result of raised intra-cranial pressure in response to trauma elsewhere.

Going deeper still, is the "brain stem" which controls the things we do without thinking, such as our heartbeat, breathing and swallowing.

Deeper still at the bottom of the brain, is the spinal cord which extends from the brain all the way to the tail bone. It is about as wide as a small finger.

CHAPTER TWO

THE CAUSES OF INJURY TO THE BRAIN

Let us get one thing clear first of all. "Head injury" does not mean "brain injury". Head injury can mean injuries not to the brain but injuries to the scalp, skull, face and jaw.

Head injury is therefore an all-encompassing term of which brain injury is a sub-set. Brain injury from trauma is normally what personal Injury lawyers are dealing with and the preferred term is "traumatic brain injury". Where we are dealing with traumatic brain injury which is not at first sight obvious or apparent then the term "STBI" or subtle traumatic brain injury can be used. It does not imply however that the brain injury is necessarily minor or is not having substantial and very serious effects upon the functioning of the individual.

Injury to the brain can however occur as a result of a number of conditions including:

- Trauma
- Cerebrovascular events
- Degenerative disorders
- Hydrocephalus
- Toxicity
- Infection

- Tumours
- Oxygen deprivation
- Metabolic and endocrine dysfunction
- Nutritional deficiencies

What is a traumatic brain injury?

The first problem is that a head injury and a brain injury are often confused. One can of course sustain an injury to the "head" without sustaining injury to the brain. There may conversely be no visible injury to the "head" yet the brain itself may have sustained an injury.

Traumatic brain injury means trauma to the brain as a result of some external force to the brain usually with some diminished or altered state of consciousness. This does not mean that somebody has to be unconscious in order to have demonstrated or suffered a brain injury.

The ICD11, one of the international diagnostic manuals used by doctors, recognises that head injury can be anything from a superficial injury to the head through to an intra-cranial injury. Intra-cranial injury can range from concussion to traumatic amputation of the head.

Traumatic Brain injury ("TBI") is global world health problem and is a major cause of disability. According to the World Health Organisation, traumatic brain injury will soon exceed many diseases as the cause of major disability and death.

In the UK there are roughly 400 incidents of traumatic head injury per 100,000 of population in any one year and around 240 per 100,000 in the EU as a whole. Overall, males are twice as likely than females to experience a TBI and the risk of traumatic brain injury is particularly high in relation to children. The mortality rate is between 5 and 10 per 100,000 in the UK.

The leading cause of traumatic brain injury is consistently reported as being road traffic accidents, around 21% in the UK and 25% in the USA.

There is some evidence that genetic factors may pre-dispose some people to a poorer outcome following such injury. Some research has shown that the apolipoprotein E has an effect on the deposit of amyloid beta-protein in the cerebral cortex and this is involved in neuro-degeneration. Some people more prone to produce this lipo-protein have been associated with a doubling of likelihood of a poorer outcome at 6 months following a traumatic brain injury.

Types of traumatic brain injury

These may be **closed or blunt** where the dura mater and brain are not penetrated.

Or **open or penetrating** where the dura and brain are penetrated.

Skull fractures or their absence are not always of significance. They do indicate that a substantial amount of force hit the head but of course the area over which the force is distributed may mean that the skull in fact fractures.

Skull fractures may result in CSF leakage however and are an important source of infection and air bubbles. The orbital roof is commonly fractured when for example a person falls backwards hitting the occiput on a hard surface with the shock wave passing through the skull and fracturing the orbital roof which is pretty thin.

Coup and contrecoup

Coup is the expected movement of the brain when for example it decelerates. The rebound movement of the brain, for example rearwards again is the contrecoup.

Haemorrhage which is intra-cranial, inside the skull can be outside the dura or inside the dura. If it is outside or above the dura (see Chapter 1) it is known as an **extradural haemorrhage.** This is as a result of a direct impact to the skull.

If it is beneath the dura it is known as a **sub-dural haemorrhage.**

It is important of course to remember that the force does not have to be applied to the skull in order for a brain injury to occur. The brain is of course for example in a motor vehicle usually moving. When it decelerates suddenly the brain continues to try and move and strikes the inside of the hard skull, the calvarium. Contusions consist of haemorrhage and can carry on bleeding for hours causing a raised intra-cranial pressure. It is a particular problem the older the person gets as the brain atrophies with age and allows for even greater movement within the skull.

Sub-dural haemorrhage which is present soon after the injury is known as "acute". If it is only present 1-2 weeks later it is called "sub-acute" and if it is present more than 2 weeks later it is called "chronic sub-dural haemorrhage".

Sub-arachnoid haemorrhage is particularly serious. This often results from an impact to the head and with contusions and lacerations. A laceration around one of the arteries feeding the brain stem often results in immediate collapse and is often fatal. It is a marker for catastrophic brain injury and consequent epilepsy.

Diffuse Injury

Diffuse Axonal Injury is altogether very different and it is very important in terms of brain injury. Diffuse axonal injury can be very serious, even fatal of course and does not necessarily equate with a subtle traumatic brain injury although is often referred to in that context.

Diffuse Axonal Injury ("DAI") is widespread damage to the axons within the brain. Trauma is an accepted cause of DAI as is hypoxia (lack of oxygen to the brain) and hypoglycaemia (lack of nutrition to the cells). DAI caused by trauma is different however, and it can be caused by rapid acceleration or deceleration of the head particularly where there is a rotational movement of the head.

Traumatic axonal Injury can cause very severe brain injury resulting in death. In these cases it causes immediate unconsciousness and can result even in persistent vegetative states (PVS). In these severe cases there will be damage to the small blood vessels resulting in spots of blood being present on the MRI scans. These are called "Petechiae" or "petechial haemorrhages".

Damage to the axons results in swollen, torn and damaged fibres in the *white matter* of the brain. Over time, damaged axons may die and there may be shrinkage of the white matter. Ironically therefore, the effects in more minor cases of DAI may take some time to become immediately apparent. Damage to these long fibres can also cause an influx of enzymes and damage to proteins disrupting axonal transport mechanisms and resulting in accumulation of proteins.

The relationship between white matter damage and the effect upon higher executive functions is proving to be very complex to medical science.

Research by Kinnuen, Greenwood and Powell et al. reported in the medical Journal, "Brain" (Brain 2011:134; 449-463) suggests that although chronic and widespread abnormalities of white matter are identifiable following traumatic brain injury, the impact of these changes on cognitive function is likely to depend on the precise damage to key pathways that link nodes in the brain network supporting high level cognitive functions.

The frontal lobe at the point where it rests on the cribriform plate (to the rear of the nasal bones) is particularly vulnerable to axonal injury from contrecoup forces following a whiplash type injury mechanism. This is the area which controls executive function and personality. The olfactory bulb, which is responsible for sense of smell surrounds it.

The Corpus Callosum

This is the largest single bundle of axons crossing over from the left to the right side of the brain and linking the two. The structure of the brain makes it prone to injury during certain types of impact, particularly rotational.

The falx is a stiff cartilage-like structure running down the fissure dividing the left and right hemispheres of the brain. At the centre of the brain is small vault-like structure known as the "central sulcus". The large bundle of axons, the corpus callosum cross over from the left to the right side of the brain deep inside the brain.

Comprehensive studies have been performed by David Camarillo and his team on American football players to measure the forces which are transmitted as a result of impacts and in particular head rotation. [1]

They used a mouthguard fitted with sensors to detect how the head actually moved when struck. This allowed them to study live subjects who commonly suffered concussion as a result of impact, namely American Football Players.

---

[1] See "Why helmets don't prevent concussion and what might". TED Talk 29th September 2016.

A player struck to the lower left side of the mask suffered a whiplash type effect. First the head went to the left and then whipped violently to the right.

Computer simulations measured the stretch on the known properties of the brain tissue.

Contrary to the expectation of surface related coup-contrecoup injuries the key thing to notice from the study is that the falx appeared to rapidly transmit the highest forces down the fissure into the central sulcus where the single largest axon bundle was. This is the corpus callosum. This caused a dissociation between the right and left side of the brain and symptoms of traumatic brain injury.

Diffuse Vascular Injury

In very severe cases of acceleration/deceleration of the brain there can be widespread petechial haemorrhaging. These injuries are generally fatal.

Persistent vegetative and minimally conscious states

These are the most severe forms of brain injury short of death. PVS and MCS are not the same.

A vegetative state (VS) will have the following characteristics:-

- Sleep/wake cycles with spontaneous eye opening;
- Preserved brain-stem function so that circulation and respiration are spontaneously maintained;
- No awareness of the environment or of themselves;
- Absence of response to sensory stimulus;

- Absence of language comprehension or meaningful expression.

If the condition lasts longer than 8 weeks it is then a persistent vegetative state ("PVS"). This does not necessarily mean that it is not reversible however.

However, once 6 months has passed then it is usually classed as permanent albeit there remains a possibility though not a probability of improvement.

A minimally conscious state differs from a vegetative State (VS) because:

- There is limited but defined awareness of the environment
- There is a sub-category of MCS minus patients and MCS plus patients
    - MCS minus show non-reflexive movements sometimes when stimulated;
    - MCS plus show more complex behaviours, following commands for example despite profound cognitive impairment.

Improvement from PVS and MCS

Age is an important factor. In relation to PVS- Patients over 40 years of age show worse improvement than those under 40 years of age. At one year according to a meta-study:-

- 33% had died
- 15% remained in a PVS

- 28% were severely disabled
- 17 % were moderately disabled
- 7% had made a good recovery.

Patients with a MCS show much more variable levels of recovery but almost all of them continue to need life-long care.

Hidden Consciousness (CMD)

The latest research from Columbia University, New York, considers that around 15% of "coma" patients may have Cognitive Motor Dissociation (CMD) but are not actually in a coma. These are patients who are processing at least some of what is happening around them but cannot physically respond. CMD is a break between understanding and responding. The diagnosis requires advanced equipment and training. The team have found however that simpler equipment can also diagnose the condition, structural MRI to look or brain lesions combined with functional EEG (Electro-encephalogram). Using both they were able to identify two patterns of brain lesions only seen in CMD patients. The lesion patterns were not surprisingly in areas of the brain important for motor output but comprehension and arousal centres of the brain were intact. CMD patients have a higher chance of recovery but there is a risk that failure to identify CMD patients could mean that life-sustaining therapies are withdrawn prematurely. The drug Amantadine has been shown to help recovery in patients in a vegetative or minimally conscious state and the next steps are trial this in patients with CMD to see if it aids recovery there too.

Summary

In summary:-

Primary brain injury is usually caused by either a direct blow to the head or more usually in our experience of acceleration/deceleration forces on the brain leading to:-

- Contusional injury (bruising of the brain)
- Coup (at the site of the impact)
- Contre-coup (at the opposing side of the impact)
- Diffuse axonal injury (DAI) which is the shearing or stretching of axons or fibres connecting neurones or nerve cells together
- Sometimes but not always haematoma or loss of blood.

After primary injury, secondary injury can occur especially in more severe head injury, as a result of oedema (swelling due to fluid), hypoxia (lack of oxygen to the nerve cells) and infection.

- PVS and MCS are the most severe forms of brain injury and generally outcomes are very poor with lifelong support needed albeit with substantially reduced life-expectancy.
- There is a concern about hidden consciousness called CMD. Up to 15% of "coma" cases may be a case of hidden consciousness with an inability to communicate but processing is still occurring.

CHAPTER THREE

SEVERE TRAUMATIC BRAIN INJURY

Glasgow Coma Scale

The Glasgow Coma Scale (GCS) was developed at the University of Glasgow in 1974. This is the most extensively used system for assessing the level of consciousness. The scale is based on the motor (M) verbal (V) and eye-opening (E) responses of the patient and is used to classify injury as "minor", "moderate" or "severe". The scale does not go to 0. The minimum score representing complete unconsciousness is 3. Traditional thinking is as follows:-

13-15 means you may be likely to be dealing with a **mild or Minor** injury.

9-12 means you may be likely to be dealing with a **moderate** injury.

Less than or equal to 8 usually means a **severe** injury.

Note that 15/15 on the GCS scale means fully conscious.

A GCS score of 3 the lowest score represents no eye opening to pain, no verbal response and no motor response to pain. This would be recorded in the notes as E1, V1, M1.

A fully conscious score of 15 would be recorded as E4, V5, M6.

It is not just the total score that matters. Claimants with the same total score but differing components of the scores can have different outcomes.

Here is a useful table which you can refer back to which shows how the GCS score is reached:-

Level	Eye response	Verbal response	Motor response
1	No eye opening	No verbal response	No motor response
2	Eye opening in response to pain	Incomprehensible sounds	Extensions to pain (e.g. extension of wrist)
3	Eye opening to speech	Inappropriate words	Abnormal flexion to pain (e.g. flexion of wrist)
4	Eyes opening spontaneously	Confused	Flexion/withdrawal to pain (e.g. pulls away when pinched)
5		Oriented to time, place and person	Localises to pain (e.g. purposeful movements towards painful stimuli)
6			Obeys commands

It is easily forgotten that there may be other signs of brain injury and in the medico-legal context there can be an over-emphasis of the importance of GCS scores.

Signs of injury on the scalp such as bruising and lacerations, depressed skull fractures, sub-conjunctival haemorrhages bleeding, and discharge of CSF from the ear or nose may be indicators of brain injury. The latter are particularly associated with skull base fractures. Anosmia or loss of the sense of smell may also be an indicator of brain injury.

It is also wrong to assume that any fall in the level of consciousness with time cannot be due to brain injury. It may be falsely associated with medical treatment. In fact, raised intra-cranial pressure may also cause a decrease in the level of consciousness over time in the aftermath of the hours after the traumatic event. The cranium is of course a rigid box containing the brain. Any increase in volume caused by blood, swelling of the brain or CSF can cause raised intra-cranial pressure and a fall in the level of consciousness. If left untreated, death may soon occur. Some severe brain injury patients therefore must have part of their skull removed to allow the brain to expand. This is called craniotomy. The reconstruction and replacement of the skull is called cranioplasty.

Some victims of brain injury are the "walking wounded". Seemingly normal at first but with a fatal or very severe outcome. This is why of course CT scanning in the accident and emergency context is extremely useful. It is being used to detect and exclude the possibility of a bleed leading to raised intra-cranial pressure and the possibility of a severe outcome or death.

The GCS-P scale

GCS-P is a newer scale developed by a team of researchers from Glasgow and Edinburgh Universities. It is an updated version of the GCS scale which aims to assist with the severity and prognosis for brain injury. It adds the reactivity of a patient's pupils as this has been found to be a key prognostic indicator. The pupil reactivity is scored 0,1 or 2, (2 being the poorest pupil reactivity). This is then subtracted from the GSC score resulting in the GCS-P score. It follows that this can then be as low as 1 or as high as 15.

The team have then developed prediction charts based on the GCS-P scale to show:-

1. Probability or chance of death;

2. Probability of a favourable outcome in patients, 6 months after the TBI.

The scale can help manage expectations for the family and can help you to decide how to approach the case.

The Mayo system

The Mayo system is a different classification system of brain injury and is less useful perhaps in severe catastrophic brain injury.

It was developed to deal with some of the difficulties arising from the use of GCS to identify a mild traumatic brain injury. The Mayo system has several main categories:-

1. Definite moderate-severe traumatic brain Injury;

2. Probable moderate traumatic brain injury

3. Possible traumatic brain injury

The scale utilises multiple criteria including loss of consciousness, post-traumatic amnesia, skull fracture and evidence of neuro-radiological abnormalities. To fall into the moderate severe category there would usually have to be loss of consciousness of 30 minutes or more and post traumatic amnesia of more than 24 hours.

The Mayo system is generally thought of as far more reliable than GCS scale score at identifying the presence brain injury but is limited by the top category being "moderate-severe".

Post-traumatic amnesia is a very important component of identifying whether there has been a brain injury and the severity of it.

Post-traumatic amnesia is the interval from injury until the patient can form and lay down and recall new memories.

One research paper by Nakase-Richardson et al (2011) concluded that:-

- a PTA of 0-14 days was classified as a moderate TBI,
- a PTA of 15-28 days was classified as a moderately severe TBI,
- and a PTA of 29-70 days or more was classified as a severe TBI.

Other factors are also taken into account including the presence of dizziness and nausea and headache.

The Mayo system of classification is multi-factorial and has been shown to be sensitive with a high degree of reliability on predicting brain injury and the outcome of it.

One problem however particularly in the in the UK is that there is usually no prospective tool used for the assessment of post-traumatic amnesia in the clinical setting. Assessments of PTA are therefore being made retrospectively. Friedland writing in an article in Spine 2013, S4, states that the retrospective analysis of post-traumatic amnesia can yield false positives in terms of diagnosing an individual as suffering from a TBI.

The "Russell" System of Classification of brain injury

The Russell system depends heavily on the level of Post traumatic amnesia and injuries are classified as follows:-

- Mild – PTA of less than 1 hour.
- Moderate – PTA of more than 1 hour but not more than 24 hours.
- Severe – PTA or more than 24 hours but not more than 1 week.
- Very severe – PTA of more than 1 week but less than 1 month.

- Extremely severe – PTA of more than 1 month.

It is difficult in a *legal* book of this size to give a comprehensive analysis. A brief summary however is as follows:- A TBI is moderate to severe if one or more features exist:-

- Loss of consciousness of 30 minutes or more.
- Post traumatic amnesia of 24 hours or more.
- The lowest GCS score in the first 24 hours is 12 or less.
- Haemorrhagic contusion, Penetrating TBI, Sub-arachnoid haemorrhage, brain stem injury, intra-cerebral haematoma, sub-dural haematoma or any of them are present.
- The length of post traumatic amnesia (the length of time before continuous memory is re-established) is one of the better indicators of traumatic brain injury.
- Abnormalities on neuro-imaging will influence the conclusion.

It is worth remembering however that there is no "gold standard" in relation to classification systems for brain injury. It is important that they are understood and the various limitations of each appreciated.

CHAPTER FOUR

NEURO-IMAGING

Imaging in the accident and emergency department is generally performed if there is suspicion of a brain injury or there are substantial neurological deficits. Acute imaging is aimed at identifying problems which need urgent surgical intervention or medical attention to alleviate further injury or death.

The most available form of useful scan is therefore the Computed Tomography or "CT" scan and it is this which is most normally available in the Claimant's medical notes. CT scans impose very high radiation doses often equivalent to 500 x-rays at once. Clinical and investigatory use has to be justified.

It has largely replaced the use of skull x-rays as it is quick and available and detailed. It identifies quickly bleeds, clotted or otherwise which require stemming or removal of clots.

If the GCS has dropped below 13 at any time since injury or is still at 13 or 14 at 2 hours post injury then the NICE guidelines suggest that scanning should be carried out. There are other elements to the criteria as well and the full criteria can be found at www.nice.org.uk.

Imaging after the acute phase

Magnetic resonance imaging or "MRI" is the imaging of choice however to reveal brain injuries. MRI does not involve any significant radiation dose. It is not used in the acute phase because it is impractical and often not available but it can be used afterwards to obtain a clearer picture of the extent of injury and in particular is much more useful in being able to detect diffuse axonal injury caused by those shearing or acceleration deceleration forces.

DAI is usually seen in the white matter, the corpus collosum and the pontine-mesencephalic junction. It is often seen at the borders of the grey cortical matter and the white matter due to the different physical properties of the grey and white matter resulting in the shearing of tissue at these points under deceleration-acceleration forces particularly rotational forces.

The imaging of choice is now at least 3T MRI examination of the brain with gradient echo and SWI (susceptibility weighted imaging) which assesses the extent of micro-bleeds and residual brain damage. The T stands for Tesla. 3T is twice as sensitive as 1.5 T MRI in detecting diffuse axonal injury.

3T MRI with SWI is the most sensitive technique available in clinical practice (some universities now have up to 7T) to detect evidence of micro-haemorrhage. These are low signal intensity lesions which occur due to the deposit of a substance called "haemosiderin". This substance has a high magnetic susceptibility so therefore shows up even in small amounts.

This is particularly important in assessing traumatic brain injury.

MRI scanning, especially 3T may be useful in visualising the extent of the catastrophic brain injury and may help with the prognosis.

Some incredible imaging of the brain can now be done. Albeit not for clinical and medico-legal use, see for example a link on the BBC Website to the most detailed scan of the brain ever, achieved by Cardiff University.

https://www.bbc.co.uk/news/av/health-40487049

Diffusion weighted imaging (DWI) and diffusion tensor imaging (DTI) may be useful. This relies on the difference between isotropic diffusion of water molecules in a normal and injured brain.

PET, Positron Emission Tomography measures the accumulation of positron emitting radioisotopes within the brain.

3T MRI scanning is likely to be the most helpful and is probably the imaging of choice as discussed before. It is conducted now in a wide range of centres, including, London and Liverpool.

White matter disruption is an important determinant of cognitive impairment after brain injury and the location of the disruption can lead a good neuro-radiologist to predict the cognitive functions likely to be impaired such as memory and higher executive functions.

The field of neuro-radiology is rapidly changing and new techniques are evolving all the time to provide more information about the extent of injury, underlying physiological changes and anatomy.

Summary:

- Post acute imaging can be helpful even in catastrophic injury cases to give a more detailed picture of the areas of brain severely injured.
- This can help with the prognosis.

CHAPTER FIVE

THE FUNCTIONS OF DIFFERENT AREAS OF THE BRAIN

The left side

The left side of the brain deals with language, movement of the right side of the body, verbal and analytical thinking, encoding of verbal information, semantic memory (knowledge and information), deductive reasoning and verbal memory.

The right side

In most people, the right side deals with some degree of language if left handed, movement of the left side of the body, visual and spatial reasoning, retrieval of information, episodic information, inductive reasoning and visual memory.

The frontal lobes and executive function

The terms frontal lobe syndrome and "dysexecutive syndrome" and organic personality disorder are often used loosely.

Executive functions are concerned with recognising that something needs to be done and with planning and initiating and regulating such behaviour.

The orbito-frontal region

This is involved with behavioural control and insight and problems include a lack of insight, impulsive behaviour, irrational behaviour, disinhibition, poor temper control, obsessive behaviour and egocentricity.

The dorso-lateral region

This is involved in cognitive problems that may include mental juggling, inefficient recall of information, reduced fluency, concrete, rigid or inflexible thinking, reduced ability to estimate.

The medial region

Damage to this region may result in problems such as a lack of drive, lack of initiative, apathy, flatting or absence of emotion.

These problems occur often in combination and with varying degrees of severity.

Effects of Head injury

Broadly there are 3 consequences to head injury

- Physical consequences
- Cognitive consequences
- Emotional Consequences

Physical consequences

The physical consequences are often clear such as the loss of sight, headaches, and other obvious physical signs. In the most severe and catastrophic traumatic brain injury cases, there will be a loss of the use of limbs, inability to walk or hold the body and spasticity. We shall see that in relation to life expectancy, the ability to walk and to be able to self-feed are important determinants of life expectancy after traumatic brain injury.

Cognitive consequences

Cognitive abilities comprise memory thinking and communicating. The most common problems are memory problems. Memory events which happen well before the injury are not usually impaired unless the injury was extremely severe and memory events which happen well before the injury are usually not badly impaired. What is common is difficulty in learning new information, retraining, and retrieving such information.

The speed with which they approach any task including cognitive tasks are therefore slower. Keeping track of more than one thing at a time. They may become overloaded and frustrated. Problems in language and communication can also be common. Forgetting names even those they could not reasonably expect to forget can occur. Concrete thinking is also common. These problems occur from damage to the frontal part of the brain. These frontal deficits can be very subtle, not evident to the casual observer and sometimes even cognitive testing does not uncover them.

Emotional consequences

Changes in emotion and behaviour are very common after more severe head injury. After recovery from initial unconsciousness, a patient within the rehabilitation setting may well display confused, abusive and uncontrolled behaviour. Sexual impropriety and inappropriate comments often directed towards staff are common. As a legal professional attending a rehabilitation setting, you should expect to see and be prepared for this. If this behaviour does not change it will impact on the care package. Risky behaviour can mean that a 2:1 support package will be required perhaps for life regardless of physical problems necessitating such a regime

CHAPTER SIX

LIABILITY

Catastrophic brain injuries bring their own unique problems in establishing and disputing liability for the accident. I wish to say at the outset that I am not an expert engineer and have relied on acquired knowledge from experts over the years. Always instruct an appropriate expert for advice and rely on their knowledge. This is a practical guide to where and when to turn to an expert.

It seems sensible to begin with a closer look at some of the practical and legal aspects of establishing liability for the accident. We cannot cover every aspect of liability or brain injury in a guide of this length.

Accidents at work (EL) and (PL) have a greater tendency to be fairly clear cut in relation to liability and often don't give rise to too many difficulties.

Stairway accidents cause many fatalities or severe and catastrophic traumatic brain injuries. I have dealt with many of those too. The key point in those cases are to try to obtain and preserve CCTV of the incident quickly.

It is outside the scope of this book to consider birth injury traumatic brain injury claims which bring their own unique challenges.

The greatest number of cases I see are in relation to road traffic claims.

There are three common methods of injury which catastrophic brain injury lawyers tend to see in the road traffic context:-

1. Pedestrian road traffic accidents.

2. Road traffic accidents involving cyclists and E-scooter users.

3. Road traffic accidents involving motorcyclists.

Severe frontal or side collisions involving car drivers are of course capable of causing severe brain injuries but perhaps thanks to the safer and more robust design of cars (see https://www.euroncap.com/en/) are becoming less common. The rules of the road usually mean that it is often fairly easy to determine fault in those claims.

In my view, severe brain injury seems to be a little less common in that scenario than in relation to the above mechanisms.

Workplaces too have become safer and catastrophic accidents involving falls are thankfully more rare

Of the above three categories, I tend to see the most severe and truly catastrophic brain injuries in relation to pedestrians and increasingly E-scooters.

All of the above three categories are however often the most difficult cases to prove in relation to liability for three reasons.

1. Firstly, it is quite common that the Claimant himself has no witness with them when crossing the road or riding their motorcycle;

2. Secondly, the Claimant themselves is either left unconscious, cognitively severely disabled or unable to speak; or both;

3. Thirdly, the Claimant has no memory of the accident due to pre-traumatic amnesia caused by the brain injury.

4. Fourthly, it is difficult to discern principles from the case law.

In these circumstances, it is very tempting to simply rely upon the recollections of apparently independent witnesses in reaching a view upon liability, but this can be unreliable and cause severe injustice.

Civil lawyers who have never practised in criminal law, would do well to remember the direction to be given to juries pursuant to *R v Turnbull* [1977] QB 224. The case related to identification evidence but may be of general application in relation to witness evidence. The Court of Appeal reminded us that:-

1. Caution is required to avoid the risk of injustice;

2. A witness who is honest may be wrong even if they are convinced they are right;

3. A witness who is convincing may still be wrong;

4. More than one witness may be wrong;

5. A witness who recognises the Defendant, even when the witness knows the Defendant very well, may be wrong.

It is also worth recognising that in civil cases, witnesses may not appreciate that blame can be shared and that accidents may not all be the fault of just one party or the other. Lay witness views tend to be very polarised and they sometimes decide liability for themselves and unwittingly or consciously take "sides".

In one catastrophic brain injury case, I successfully sought approval of the compromise reached upon liability at 65% in favour of the Claimant, in the High Court. No fewer than four witnesses had blamed the Claimant <u>entirely</u> for the accident. The police had declined to prosecute the driver and the driver had exculpated himself by suggesting he had been driving at no more than 25 mph on approach to the accident scene.

The Claimant had little or no memory of the accident and lacks mental capacity. The accident had occurred on or near to a pedestrian crossing where the lights were green in favour of the car driver. There was no doubt that the Claimant did not look properly or at all in crossing the road.

No fewer than four firms of solicitors had wrongly advised the Claimant that there were less than reasonable prospects of success. The fifth firm were more savvy and instructed me to consider the CCTV they, or the police, had secured from a local shop overlooking the accident scene.

I did a rough and ready analysis in conference using a stopwatch and some simple video viewing software and concluded that this Defendant was probably driving at least 34 mph in a 30 mph limit in busy complex conditions in the wet on approach to a traffic light controlled pedestrian crossing.

Incidentally, there is a very useful speed, distance time calculator created by "Calculator Soup". It can be found here at the time of writing.

https://www.calculatorsoup.com/calculators/math/speed-distance-time-calculator.php

If you want to understand the formula, it is as follows:

Distance = Speed x Time
Time = Distance / Speed
Speed = Distance / Time

There was every reason to suspect that the accident would never have occurred if the driver had indeed been driving at less than 30 mph as in fact he indicated he was doing when interviewed by the police. This was a lie or at least a gross error.

We commissioned a detailed CCTV report and then a road traffic accident reconstruction report. In fact, this revealed that the Defendant was driving at between 37 and 38 mph, a fact with which, eventually, the Defendant's insurers had to agree.

The accident would never have occurred even though the Claimant had taken less care in crossing the road than they should have done. The point is that all four witnesses were mistaken. None of them blamed the Defendant at all for the accident or said that the speed of the vehicle was excessive. The case settled at a good seven figure sum.

It is of real concern that the legal system nearly failed this Claimant.

The point is that there is much that can be done from an analysis point of view even where you lack reliable witness evidence to determine what happened and as a check against that witness evidence.

There are four principal methods of reconstruction. Two methods of reconstruction are common. And there is an emerging fifth method of reconstruction.

1. **CCTV** -The first and most reliable evidence is usually CCTV evidence either from surrounding road traffic system cameras used to control the traffic or from the car itself or from buildings around the scene of the accident. This can be used to determine the speed of the vehicle on approach and prior to impact as well as the actions of the driver and pedestrian or motorcyclist or cyclist as the case may be.

2. **Pedestrian throw** – the second, but usually less reliable reconstruction evidence can be from a pedestrian throw calculation which can be used to determine the speed of the vehicle at impact;

3. **Physical evidence** – the third, can be from physical evidence from the vehicle(s) themselves or evidence left or deposited on

the road. An example might be skid marks (although less common now that cars are fitted with anti-lock braking systems).

Sometimes a combination of the above evidence will be used to reconstruct the accident.

4. **Electronic evidence** – The fourth from electronic systems within the vehicle such as the electronic control unit or "black box" which may hold data such as speed and G forces sustained in a collision.

A new and emerging technique which is potentially very exciting is being performed by a team at a London University. I will call it "advanced analytics".

5. **Advanced analytics** – the potential for real-time prediction and assessment of the likelihood or cause of traumatic brain injury using sensor technology and data analysis from the scene of the accident and MRI scanning. This was used in at least one case to determine whether the brain injury pattern seen in a cyclist found unconscious on a roundabout was caused by being struck by a motor car. The driver claimed innocence and that the Claimant simply fell from his bicycle. It was established that the driver had indeed struck the cyclist and he had not simply fallen. The same team can also analyse the difference, if any, that a cycle helmet would have made in a particular accident.

CCTV Evidence

A modern "closed-circuit television system" or "CCTV" consists of a number of cameras connected to a digital recorder which records the footage on to a hard drive. The footage can then normally be copied either onto a data CD or DVD or USB memory stick together with proprietary software enabling the footage to be viewed on a normal computer.

Most CCTV cameras produce 25 images per second. This is therefore not the same as a television which produces at least 60 images per second. There is usually a constant time period of 0.04 seconds in between the consecutive images. If all of these images are recorded the footage is called “real-time” footage. In some cases however the camera system only records a proportion of the images which allows for better usage of space on the hard drive. This is known as “time lapse” CCTV footage.

Hard drive recorders do not necessarily record time lapse footage at a constant rate so the time intervals between consecutive images can vary. However, because vehicle speeds change only gradually in the short time intervals between the consecutive CCTV images it is possible to calculate the time intervals between the CCTV images by using the vehicle movements. The average speed of a vehicle between two CCTV images can then be calculated provided that the time interval and the distance travelled between those two images can be established.

One problem that can occur is that when CCTV footage is not preserved on the original hard drive and it is downloaded to, say, a DVD-video, images can be lost and the image quality reduced when the CCTV footage is converted from its original format into DVD-video format.

It is therefore very important for a Solicitor when presented with a catastrophic injury claim where footage may exist, to act very quickly to advise or secure or preserve the original footage. The police can not always be relied upon to secure or preserve the original footage. Furthermore, most CCTV footage will be lost if active steps are not taken within at least 3 months of the accident date to secure the original footage.

One method of seeking to preserve the footage is to seek undertakings say from the local authority or police or an individual to secure the footage. On other occasions an interim order for the preservation of property may be specifically required. In one case, we secured an undertaking for the CCTV footage to be preserved and then sent our CCTV expert to the local authority offices to ensure that the footage was downloaded and preserved so that no images were lost or degraded. In this particular case, this proved crucial to securing a settlement at around 75% of the value of the case. The case was borderline and we won only because my solicitors instructed me early and acted on my advice quickly to secure the footage within the first 3 months after the accident.

Pedestrian throw calculation

Pedestrians and cyclists behave in similar ways when struck by a motor vehicle. There are ways in which the speed of the vehicle can be found from the evidence at the scene of the accident. Some methods require the distance the person was thrown, whilst others use the spread of debris or the position of the head strike. Much will depend upon who visited the scene after the accident and the precision with which recording and preservation of the evidence was made. For this reason, it is always vital to ascertain not just whether there was a police report but whether the collision accident investigator attended the scene, made a full and detailed report and took video or photographs of the evidence.

In order to perform a pedestrian-throw calculation it is necessary to know the Claimant's height and weight and what clothes they were wearing.

Next, the way in which the pedestrian was struck can tell us quite a lot about the accident and potential speed of the vehicle even before an expert is instructed.

There are basically four ways in which a pedestrian can be struck.

1. The fender vault;
2. The forward vault.
3. The wrap vault;
4. The roof vault;

The fender vault

This is where the pedestrian has been struck by one corner of the vehicle. The pedestrian tends to slide across the wing. The pedestrian does not tend to receive the full strike of the motor car and is unlikely to be accelerated to the same speed as the motor car. Any calculated speed from a pedestrian throw calculation is unlikely to be a true estimate of speed. It is likely to be an under-estimate of speed. The body is often deflected to the side of the vehicle and is likely to come to rest behind the vehicle.

The evidence can help to tell us whether the person walked or ran in front of the vehicle. If the person is walking towards the car it is possible to find a head strike on the windscreen as the upper body continues to move across the car despite the wing pushing the lower body away. The head strike is normally to one side of the windscreen. It would be wrong to assume that the injuries cannot be very severe just because the body does not undergo acceleration to the full speed of the striking vehicle. One of the worst cases I have known was a fender vault strike at only 26 mph. The unfortunate catastrophically injured Claimant was thrown into the air and rotated and landed on his head. The speed limit was 20 mph and if it had been obeyed no accident would have occurred. The speed turned the initial impact into a roof vault collision (see below).

If the pedestrian was running across the road and into the car you often get crush damage to the side of the wing caused by the pedestrian and the head strike is further across the windscreen. As the speed of the vehicle increases the head strike tends to rise further up the windscreen.

Forward vault

This sort of impact usually occurs when the pedestrian is struck by a predominantly large and flat fronted vehicle such as a bus or goods vehicle. It can be seen when a pedestrian particularly a child is struck by a large off-road type vehicle.

The pedestrian undergoes a very high rate of acceleration and is thrown horizontally away from the vehicle. A pedestrian throw calculation is therefore quite useful.

The wrap vault

The pedestrian in this case is usually being struck around the centre of the vehicle and wraps himself over the front profile of the vehicle. The lower legs make contact with the bumper of the car. The upper legs and waist then roll over the leading edge of the bonnet. The abdomen and chest then fall onto the upper area of the bonnet. The mechanism is speed dependent.

At lower speeds the shoulders and head will strike the upper edge of the bonnet of the windscreen. As the speed increases this can push the position of the head strike further up the windscreen. There is usually a path of contact marks on the vehicle from the bonnet up to the windscreen which tells the story.

Dirty cars will also show even more as clothing wipes away the dirt on the surface. These are called "cleaning marks". Even clean cars will often reveal scratches to the paintwork particularly when viewed carefully in different lighting conditions and at different angles.

Preservation of the original vehicles in the accident rather than just police photographs can be very useful.

Roof vault

As the impact speeds increase it is possible for the body to rotate in the air as it disengages from the impact. Much then depends upon the reaction of the driver. It is possible for the pedestrian to remain suspended in the air whilst the car passes underneath. There is then often a secondary impact to a flailing arm or leg resulting in damage to the roof rail. This mechanism may be a sign of excessive speed (depending on the speed limit for the road involved).

A careful examination of the vehicle itself can also reveal skin deposits (see as white powder marks) and of course blood and hair deposited on the vehicle itself.

Motorcycle leathers can leave seam stitch marks on the vehicle and buttons and belts and buttons can leave gouge marks.

Calculating the speed

Pedestrian throw calculations are open to doubt for all manner of reasons. Broadly speaking however it is possible within certain parameters of error to calculate the speed of the vehicle if the distance the pedestrian is thrown from impact to point of rest is known. The point of rest can usually be determined from debris and photographs or blood on the road. The point of impact can be more difficult to determine. Other methods use the distance the body has slid after landing. An estimate of impact speed can sometimes be made from the position the head has travelled up the windscreen.

Conclusion

The important points for the Solicitor or other legal professional are to appreciate the points concerned and ensure that there is not just an over-reliance on the witnesses in such collisions.

The evidence from the scene can be determinative in an investigation into liability and should be preserved quickly where possible. As some of the examples above show however even where it has not been preserved, photographs and even downloaded CCTV can help to establish liability in cases where otherwise there would be substantial injustice.

Summary:

- Consider the physical evidence at the scene.
- Make early attempts to preserve the physical evidence.
- CCTV is often going to be the most reliable and useful evidence upon liability in a catastrophic brain injury claim due to the inability of the Claimant to tell you anything.
- The original CCTV is going to be very important as transferring the original to a different medium can change or weaken the evidence.
- Consider the early instruction of a road traffic reconstruction E
- expert and seek Counsel's advice in conference before you do.
- There are some interesting and exciting techniques of reconstruction and injury prediction on the horizon.

- Consider electronic analysis of the car's systems. You may need the help of the manufacturer to do so which can be difficult to secure without the help of the police.

CHAPTER SEVEN

PEDESTRIAN ACCIDENTS

In this chapter, I will take a closer look at some of the case-law and in particular some examples of how the higher Courts determine liability for collisions between pedestrians and vehicles. I will draw conclusions on principle from this difficult area of law and try to categorise cases. Why have I chosen pedestrian collisions? We tend to get catastrophic brain injuries in these collisions because pedestrians are the least protected. After all, they are obviously not wearing head protection.

Secondly, they are the most difficult cases in which to predict the liability outcome.

Once you have a high-quality accident reconstruction report you will be in a better position to judge whether you will or will not establish primary liability for the accident.

In *Chan v Paters & Advantage Insurance* [2021] EWHC 2994 (QB) Cavanagh J, cited with approval a summary of the law set out by HHJ Stephen Davies sitting as a High Court Judge in *AB v Main* [2015] EWGC 3183 QB. The summary adopted in Chan is at paragraphs 15-26 and contains a distillation of a number of cases.

Chan v Peters

Chan v Peters & Advantage Insurance is being relied upon more and more in cases of this type. Chan, was a 17-year old claimant outside a school. There were 2 friends on the opposite side of the road who waved to him. He emerged from behind a Vauxhall Zafira.

The Defendant had been driving at 25 mph not covering the brake and didn't slow down as he passed the school but it wasn't the end of the school day. The speed limit was 30 mph.

The Court found that Chan had jogged out from behind a parked Vauxhall Zafira giving only 0.6 seconds of reaction time to the driver. Chan collided with the nearside wheelarch. The Claimant failed to establish any liability.

The real issue was whether this was a category 1 case or category 2 case in my system below. Essentially the Court decided that this was not the end of the school day and the waving of students towards each other on the other side of the road was not sufficient to place the driver on notice so as to take reasonable precautions. The driver was therefore not negligent.

The summary adopted in Chan is at paragraphs 15-26 and contains a distillation of a number of cases.

These are the points:-

1. It is for the Claimant to establish on the balance of probabilities that the Defendant was negligent.

2. The standard of care is that of a reasonably careful driver armed with the common sense and experience of the way in which pedestrians and children in particular are likely to behave.

3. If a real risk of danger of a pedestrian emerging into the path of the vehicle was or should have been apparent to the driver, then **extraordinary precautions** should be taken BUT **if the danger was no more than a mere possibility, which would not have occurred to a reasonable driver, then there is no obligation to take extraordinary precautions.**

AB v Main

The Claimant was aged 8 years 10 months old. He suffered a catastrophic brain injury. He ran out into the road in Hale Liverpool io a collision with a care driven by the Defendant. Liability was wholly denied. The Defendant said he was travelling at 25-30 mph. The Judge found that he couldn't place any real weight on the Defendant's evidence.

In this case the Judge found that:-

- The Defendant had seen the boys by themselves
- It was obvious they were 7–9 years old
- They were engaged in play
- D Saw the Claimant move towards the centre of the pavement
- Failed to see the Claimant looking at traffic coming the other way
- Despite this, the Defendant maintained her speed at about 30 mph.

The Defendant did not cover the brakes.

In Main, the judge adopted dicta of Dame Janet Smith in *O'Connor v Stuttard* [2011] EWCA Civ 829 that there is an "exacting burden" on motorists who drive close to children playing on the pavement. A motorist in that situation has a duty to ensure whether by using his horn or otherwise that the children are aware of his presence before going past them.

The imposition of this exacting duty is justified by the fact that children are particularly vulnerable pedestrians whose actions are unpredictable.

The case suggests that if you see young children playing on the side of the road, move towards the pavement and fail to look at traffic, then a reasonably competent driver will back off the accelerator, reduce speed and cover the brake and move to a safer position towards the centre of the road without crossing the white line. Judgment for the Claimant was 80% with 20% contributory negligence.

Distillation of the proper test

It is submitted that a duty to take "extraordinary precautions" to avoid an accident arises where there is a **real risk as opposed to a mere possibility that** a pedestrian may suddenly move into the Defendant's path.

This has led me to formulate my three categories for pedestrian liability which are as follows. The cases are merely illustrative of the principles.

1. **Cases where it was only a mere possibility that the Claimant would suddenly move in front of the Defendant's motor vehicle – The Claimant will probably lose or there will be a high degree of contributory negligence.**

This can be demonstrated by the following case. It is striking because the Claimant was crossing on a pedestrian crossing. In *Kayser v London Passenger Transport Board* [1950] 1 All ER 231, 114 JP 122 this case involved an accident on a pedestrian crossing. The Claimant who was crossing in front of a bus was apparently out of the way of the bus who began to pull off expecting the Claimant to carry on crossing out of harms way. The Claimant however then reversed their direction of walking possibly due to traffic coming from the other direction and ran back in front of the bus. The bus driver had set off very slowly in first gear and his view of the Claimant was obstructed. In these circumstances the bus company escaped liability.

In *Brophy v Shaw* (1965) Times, 25 June the Claimant at night darted out into the road which was a dual carriageway. The Defendant was driving his car at about 30mph keeping close to the offside. He failed to see the men crossing from his left, until they had substantially crossed the road. The pedestrians then ran right across the front of the Defendant's vehicle resulting in a collision. The Claimant was seriously injured and his friend was killed. The Court held that the Defendant was not liable.

In *Barlow v Entwistle* 15 May 2000, Court of Appeal, Roach LJ, Latham LJ, reported in Lawtel, the Claimant was larking about on the grass beside an "A" road with two of his friends. The Claimant ran out into the road heading for the other side. The Claimant was then struck by the Defendant's car which was travelling at about 25mph. At first instance it was held that the Defendant had failed to keep a proper look out as he had not seen any pedestrians prior to impact. Therefore the Defendant was liable with contributory negligence assessed at 50%.

The Court of Appeal held that no driver could anticipate that the Claimant would, without warning or reason, run across this busy road. As such, the Defendant's failure to keep a proper look out was not a causative factor of the accident and the accident would have happened even if the Defendant had seen the Claimant and his friends. The appeal was therefore allowed and the Defendant was not liable.

In *Roda Sam (previously Al-Sam) v Atkins* [2005] EWCA Civ 1452 the claim arose following a road traffic accident on 12 February 2001, on a busy four lane street. It was dark although streetlights were on. The Claimant, a pedestrian, intended to cross from the south side of the road onto the north side. The Defendant travelling west in the offside lane was in the process of overtaking a transit van which was stationary in the nearside lane. The Defendant was travelling at no more than 20mph when the Claimant stepped out into her path from the front of a stationary transit van, and was struck by the Defendant's vehicle.

At first instance, the Judge found that although the Defendant had been negligent, this was not the cause of the accident, and dismissed the claim. The Claimant appealed. The Court of Appeal upheld the decision. The Defendant had not been negligent. The Judge was right to find in her favour, and dismissed the appeal.

In Stewart v Glaze [2009] EWHC 704 (QB) the Claimant who had been out drinking with a friend, was seriously injured when he suddenly ran out into the path of the Defendant's vehicle, resulting in a collision. The court had to determine whether the Defendant's driving fell below the standard of a reasonably competent driver. On the evidence, the Claimant had suddenly got up in the middle of a conversation with his friend, and walked towards the kerb without warning. There was nothing in the Claimant's actions, to alert the Defendant to the fact that he would run out into the path of his vehicle, especially as the Claimant was at a bus stop, with the inference that he was waiting for a bus. Therefore, the Defendant had no reason to brake, as he did not consider the Claimant to be a hazard, or potential hazard.

There was no evidence that the Defendant was speeding, and therefore he was not negligent.

In *Walford (Deceased) v London General Transport Service Ltd v Mengha* [2013] EWHC 1367 a pedestrian and a bus came into collision. In this case the Claimant failed to look for traffic before stepping onto a pedestrian crossing and the bus driver also failed to make proper checks. However, the bus driver's negligence was not causative of the accident as experts agreed that the pedestrian stepped into the road at such a late stage that the bus driver would not have had any opportunity to avoid the accident. The experts were agreed that once the Claimant stepped into the road the collision was inevitable. There would have been insufficient time for him to respond to the sound of the horn and remount the pavement. A sounding of the horn at the appropriate point would therefore not have avoided the collision, which had been caused by the Claimant's failure to look to his right before stepping into the road.

In *Boyce v Commissioner of Police of the Metropolis* [2013] EWHC 395 a drunken pedestrian was knocked down by a police car travelling marginally over the speed limit. But because the pedestrian moved onto the road at the last moment a collision was unavoidable. Further there was no evidence to state what the injuries would have been had the police car been driving at the speed limit. The case shows the importance of covering all bases in obtaining sufficient expert evidence upon causation.

It was a counsel of perfection to require any motorist to treat pedestrians on the pavement in the early hours of the morning as an actual as opposed to a potential hazard in the absence of particular features such as obvious drunkenness or horseplay.

In *Scott v Davigan* [2016] EWCA Civ 544 the Court of Appeal upheld the Judge's decision that the Claimant pedestrian was entirely to blame as he had been in an alcohol-induced state and had run across the road. The Claimant had run at an angle in front of the Defendant's moped and there was no reason to foresee the Claimant's behaviour. The Defendant had been riding at 30 mph and in the circumstances this was not negligent.

2. **Cases where there was a real risk that the Claimant would suddenly move in front of the Defendant's motor car. The Claimant is highly likely to establish a high proportion of liability**.

The following cases illustrate the principle.

In *Liddell v Middleton* [1996] PIQR P36 for example, the Claimant and his wife were attempting to cross Holderness Road, Hull at 11.45 at night. The weather was fine and dry and the road was well lit. There were gaps in the traffic. The Claimant and his wife reached the centre of the road in safety and both waited there for about ten seconds. The Claimant's wife said she saw a car coming in the distance and ran across the remaining half of the road to the opposite pavement. The Claimant did not immediately follow but waited, took one or two steps and was hit by the offside front corner of the Defendant's car. The Claimant was prevented by his injuries from giving evidence. The Defendant's evidence was that he was travelling in a line of cars, never saw the Claimant, never saw the Claimant's wife and the first thing he knew of the accident was when there was a "bang". The Judge found that the Claimant and his wife were there to be seen in the centre of the road and that the Defendant should have seen them, was driving too fast and should have sounded his horn. The Judge held the Defendant 75% to blame and the Claimant 25% contributory negligent. The Defendant appealed. The Court of Appeal held that the Defendant had failed to keep a proper look out. Furthermore, had he seen these pedestrians, the Defendant, on his own admission, would have altered the manner of his driving by slowing his speed and steering further to the nearside. Had he done so the accident would have been avoided. However, the judge was wrong to conclude that the Defendant should have sounded his horn simply if he had seen the Claimant standing in the middle of the road. As to the apportionment of liability, both parties were to blame. The Claimant's action in attempting to cross the carriageway when he did was an extremely dangerous one. The car was almost upon him and in the circumstances it gave the Defendant very little opportunity to avoid the accident. The Judge's apportionment of 25% contributory negligence was wrong in principle and too lenient. Liability was apportioned on a 50/50 basis on appeal.

In *Eagle v Chambers* [2003] EWCA Civ 1107 however, the Court of Appeal took the opportunity to enunciate the principles governing liability in collisions between pedestrians and cars. The Claimant who was 17 years at the time of the accident was walking along unsteadily in the centre of a dual carriageway. She was in a highly emotive state. The Defendant who was travelling along at 35mph struck the Claimant causing severe injuries. The Defendant failed a roadside breath test, although when retested at the station was found to be below the legal limit.

At first instance, the Claimant was found to be 60% responsible for the accident and her damages were reduced accordingly. The Claimant appealed.

The Court of Appeal per Hale LJ as she then was, held that it was

> "***rare for a pedestrian to be found more culpable than a driver unless it could be shown that she moved suddenly into the driver's path***".

As there was no evidence that the Claimant had done this, the court adopted the traditional approach in placing a higher burden on the driver particularly as a car has more destructive potential. The court held the drivers conduct was more blameworthy than that of the Claimant, although there was sufficient evidence to justify a finding of contributory negligence. The Claimant's contributory negligence was therefore reduced to 40%.

The Court of Appeal in *Adjei v King* [2003] EWCA Civ 414 again found a pedestrian attempting to cross a dual carriageway 40% contributorily negligent.

The Defendant was travelling at a speed of 25mph before he started to skid. The speed limit was 30mph. The judge felt that the Defendant was travelling too fast for the conditions and that had he been travelling slower the accident could have been avoided.

In *Green v Bannister* [2003] EWCA Civ 1819 the Claimant had collapsed in a drunken stupor in the roadway of a residential cul-de-sac outside his parent's house.

The Defendant had reversed from a parking space outside her home in the cul-de-sac, looking over her right shoulder. She continued to reverse for about 35 yards, before running over the Claimant.

The Court at first instance found in favour of the Claimant, but with a deduction of 60% to reflect contributory negligence. The Defendant appealed on the basis that the trial judge was applying a driving standard of perfection. The Court of Appeal rejected the appeal. The driver ought to have looked in her side mirrors and if she had done so would have seen the Claimant lying in the road.

In *Parkinson v Chief Constable of Dyfed Powys Police* [2004] EWCA Civ 802, the Court of Appeal refused permission to appeal where the Judge held the Claimant 35% contributorily negligent when under the influence of alcohol he stepped into the road in front of a police car travelling at 40 mph. It was a built-up area and it was night-time. The Defendant's officer should have anticipated that there may be pedestrians under the influence of alcohol given the time and area and adjusted his speed accordingly.

In *Belka v Prosperini* [2011] EWCA Civ 623 the Claimant, a pedestrian was struck by the Defendant taxi driver as he attempted to cross a dual carriageway. The collision occurred in the early hours of the morning when the Claimant was on an unregulated crossing of a dual carriageway of the A 193. Although pedestrians were entitled to cross at this point, they did not have precedence over vehicles.

Instead of waiting for the Defendant to pass, the Claimant took a chance and ran out into the path of the Defendant's vehicle resulting in a collision. Liability was apportioned 1/3 – 2/3 in favour of the Defendant, and the Claimant appealed.

The Defendant could be criticised for failing to take his foot off the accelerator as a precaution that the pedestrian may decide to cross the road in an untoward manner. However, as the Claimant attempted to cross the road in front of a vehicle that had the right of way, he was more to blame for the accident. Therefore the judge's apportionment of blame could not be criticised and the appeal was dismissed.

In *Hickman v London Central Bus Company Ltd* [2013] EWHC 1703 the Court was faced with a situation where a Claimant crossed a road, not at a pedestrian crossing, and wrongly assuming that the traffic was halted by traffic lights. However the bus driver failed to make proper checks before pulling away. In such circumstances the bus driver was 60% to blame. The High Court held that a failure to see something was not necessarily negligent. A reasonably careful driver could reasonably not have seen H it could not be negligent for D not to have done so. However, that was not the situation in the instant case.

3. **If the presence of children was or should have been obvious to the driver, then drivers should be prepared for children to be less careful than adults.**

Children's actions are not judged by the same standards as adults.

Paramasivan v Wicks [2013] EWCA Civ 262 concerned a driver who should have seen a group of youngsters and adjusted his speed. The Claimant was 13 however and not a young child. There was no indication that the child would run into the road. The trial judge had found that 25 mph was too fast and the Defendant ought to have been driving at 15 mph. He held that both parties were equally to blame.

The Court of Appeal overturned the trial Judge's decision of an equal contribution to the accident. The majority of the blame (75%) lay with the pedestrian who had gone into the road at the last moment making a collision unavoidable.

In *Ellis v Kelly* [2019] EWHC 2031 (Yip J) an 8-year old child allowed to use a playground without supervision who ran across a road and was struck by a speeding vehicle was not contributorily negligent for his injuries. His previous experience was that cars would stop at pedestrian crossings and at his age he was unable to judge that the car was travelling too fast to stop. A contribution claim against the child's mother also failed and the case is worth reading on those grounds alone although outside the scope of this chapter.

The Judgment reveals some of the factors that the Court will look at in such circumstances:-

- The age of the Claimant. Younger children tend to be more impulsive and can be taken to have lesser awareness of road safety but there is no hard and fast rule at what age a child can be found guilty of contributory negligence however age 9-10 appears to be a common age below which contributory negligence is unlikely. (20% contributory negligence in AB v Main for a child, almost 9).

- The standard of care to be taken by the child is to be judged by the reasonable expectations of a child of the same age, intelligence and experience.

- Distance from the road. The group had been quite a way from the lane in which the Defendant was driving,

- Physical separation. The group had been separated by a pavement, parking bay and the northbound carriageway,

- Predictability. There was nothing to suggest that they were about to leave that safe area and run across the road. The boys were not small infants running indiscriminately, and had provided no reason to require every driver passing by to reduce his speed to as low as 15 mph.

- No hindsight. There was a danger in the liberal use of hindsight, and a pedestrian's safety was not guaranteed.

- The driver is not to be judged by the standards of an ideal driver nor with the benefit of 20/20 hindsight.

Two more recent cases:

In *FLR v Chandran* [2023] All ER (D) (Jul) the Claimant aged 12 was held 40% contributorily negligent for failing to exercise due care when walking on a pedestrian crossing.

In *Barrow v Merrett* [2023] RTR 1 an 11-year old was run over crossing the road outside his house. The case turned on eyewitness evidence and the Defendant was found not liable.

A good question to ask is what factors made it predictable that this Claimant would emerge into the road suddenly in front of the driver.

4. **Drivers should be prepared for drunken pedestrians to be less careful.**

In *Robert Ian Ayres v Maehshodedra* [2013] EWHC 40 (QB) a motorist was primarily liable for a road traffic accident in a pedestrianised city centre zone in which he had run over a pedestrian who had stopped in front of his car, since he should have waited until the pedestrian was safely out of his way before attempting to pass him. The pedestrian was held to be only 20 per cent contributorily negligent because of his drunken state and the fact that he had dropped his trousers had hampered his ability to move freely and at normal speed out of the vehicle's path.

It is submitted that relevant factors will often be:-

- The time of day – drivers should be prepared for pedestrians later at night to be under the influence of alcohol. If it was a festival day or celebrative day such as St. Patrick's day, this would probably be a relevant factor.

- The location. Was it near to a pub, club or in a busy pedestrianised zone or city centres.

- Indication of intoxication. Could a Claimant be reasonably seen to be intoxicated by reason of unsteadiness on their feet.

All of these factors really go to whether it is reasonable to take extraordinary precautions.

Difficulty in applying these principles and litigation risk

The difficulty in applying these principles and predicting what a Court will do can be seen in a recent case of mine in the Leeds High Court of Justice (Gosnell HHJ) *Miah v Dr Hayley Jones* [2024] EWHC 92 KB. This was a case which fell into category 1 rather than 2 as we had hoped. William Waldron KC and I represented the very severely injured Claimant. There are no facts here not already in the public domain.

The accident occurred on the left northern side of the carriageway as shown in the pictures in the judgment.

This was a rural road in Wales. A bus had dropped the Claimant off at night and in darkness on the right side of the photo and the Claimant proceeded to cross the road from right to left, towards the Indian Restaurant on the left.

The bus however was bright and visible and there was a good line of sight approaching the scene of 390 metres as shown below looking towards the scene. The red arrow below is the start of the 390 metre or so line of sight to the accident scene.

The Defendant driving her mini motor car after a 14-hour work shift as a hospital doctor never mentioned either to the police or in her evidence seeing the bus. Indeed she admitted she never saw it. She also admitted in cross examination that ***if she had seen the bus she would have regarded it as a hazard and slowed right down***. She was in fact driving at 60 mph, the maximum limit for the road in conditions of darkness approaching a stopped bus opposite an Indian restaurant.

The Claimant had been almost across the road and to safety when he was struck by the left side of the Defendant's motor Mini motor car.

However it was accepted on all sides that the Claimant had not looked adequately or at all before crossing the road and the Defendant's car was there to be seen if he had done so.

We contended that this was a case for considerable contributory negligence (so within the category 2 type of case) but that a reasonably competent motorist should have heeded the stopped bus and the likelihood of pedestrians having alighted from the bus who would foreseeably cross the road. The slightest reduction in speed would have avoided the accident.

The presence of the stopped bus which the Defendant's car had passed immediately before the collision, the indicators, the bus interior lights coming on and going off again as the Claimant departed the bus, were sufficient to put the Defendant on notice that a pedestrian as is so often the case would emerge from behind it. Indeed, the Highway Code warns of this very situation.

The Court found that this was a counsel of perfection and there was no reason why the Defendant should have taken extraordinary precautions and slowed down on approach to the bus as it was difficult for a motorist to know that the bus had been stopped despite it being stopped for around four seconds and indicating left then right and pulling away, and passing the Defendant's motor car.

So, in the absence of being able to see the pedestrian (who was obscured by the bus) the mere presence of a bus opposite the restaurant or in the vicinity of it was insufficient to put the driver on notice to take extraordinary precautions. She was therefore entitled to continue driving at 60 mph or so past the bus and the restaurant and in colliding with Mr Miah, she did so entirely because of Mr Miah's failure to look as he crossed the road.

This case goes to show that there is often considerable uncertainty in whether these cases fall into a particular category and that findings of fact are key. Litigation risk is a very real factor in these cases.

The advantage at least was that a split trial meant that the economic cost of the trial was kept to a reasonable minimum and we are slightly comforted by the fact that we know that we made every possible effort for the Claimant. There were no offers forthcoming from the Defendant. Sometimes you have to fight the fight! Most of the time we win, occasionally, you will lose.

The Judgment is well worth a read anyway.

Conclusions on Main, Chan and Miah

What I take away from Main, Chan and the Miah case is that Judges are likely to decide in favour of a Claimant where the Claimant who moves suddenly into the path of a vehicle could be seen in advance of them doing so and there were reasons why a reasonably competent driver should have formed the view there was a real risk they would move in front of the vehicle.

In Chan and Miah, the pedestrian Claimant could not be seen in advance. Their presence had to be anticipated.

Courts are not likely to find that the presence of a pedestrian ought to have been anticipated except perhaps at designated crossing points giving precedence to pedestrians such as a pedestrian crossing or in a pedestrian zone and not necessarily even then.

A Court is probably going to decide against the Claimant where the Claimant ***was hidden from view by an object, whether it be a bus or a parked car until it was too late to avoid them and their presence is unlikely to be inferred from the circumstantial evidence.***

It is a Counsel of perfection to expect a driver to predict the presence of pedestrians that cannot be seen let alone suggest that they will then move in front of your vehicle.

In order to be on notice of the danger a reasonably competent driver does not have to advert to the mere risk of pedestrians stepping into the road unless you can see them or ought to have seen them. The allurement of another group of students even if they were waving at something (and no doubt the Claimant's Counsel said, obviously this must have been another friend, the Claimant) or the allurement of a restaurant on the other side of the road opposite a stopped bus is just not enough to put a reasonably competent driver on notice that a pedestrian would emerge into the path of the vehicle.

After all, young Mr Chan may have emerged suddenly and looked and stopped. Indeed he should have done so.

Mr Miah would have appeared suddenly from behind the bus and surprised Dr Jones. But, he too could have stopped and avoided the accident.

However in Main, the driver could see the children playing and failed to heed no fewer than ***seven*** clear signs that the child Claimant had not seen the oncoming car and was going to emerge in front of the Defendant's vehicle.

This is why precisely in my opinion why AB won and Chan and Miah lost. AB was also a youngish child who should be known to be unpredictable.

Contributory Negligence

Many accidents involve a degree of contributory negligence by the pedestrian. Once primary liability is admitted, the burden shifts to the Defendant to prove contributory negligence.

It is often thought to be difficult to predict contributory negligence with accuracy as there is a wide margin of discretion given to the trial judge. The decision in 2003 of the Court of Appeal in the case of *Karen Janet Eagle v Garth Maynard Chambers* [2003] EWCA Civ 1107 probably represents the highpoint of liability towards pedestrians by car drivers. The high duty in that case has probably been softened since that time but it remains good law.

In that case, the Court of Appeal highlighted the destructive potential of a motor car likening it to a dangerous weapon.

The Court will apply the Law Reform (Contributory Negligence) Act 1945. Two key factors must be considered: -

1. Blameworthiness
2. Causative potency.

In *Sabir v Nana Osei-Kwabena* [2015] EWCA Civ 1213 the Court of Appeal gave guidance upon how these principles are to be balanced. The Claimant got out of her car parked a few metres beyond a pedestrian crossing. She looked, mis-judged the distance of an approaching car and proceeded to cross the road in front of it. She was four metres into the carriageway when she was struck by the oncoming vehicle. She suffered a very significant traumatic brain injury. The Judge found the Claimant 25% responsible for the accident but the greater share of liability upon the Defendant who had not paid proper attention to the road. The Court of Appeal upheld the trial Judge but stated:-

> ***"For my part bearing in mind that the 1945 Act speaks of responsibility for the damage rather than responsibility for the accident, I am inclined to think that it is because of the destructive potential of the car driven at even moderate speed that it is "rare indeed" for a pedestrian to be found more responsible than a driver unless the pedestrian has***

> ***suddenly moved into the path of an oncoming vehicle... The proper approach I would suggest, is that the destructive capacity of a driven car comes into both aspects of the evaluation"***

Finally, even appeal Courts differ in their views.

In *Jackson v Murray* UKSC 5 the Supreme Court observed that there is no precise formulation and that contributory negligence is a somewhat "rough and ready" exercise. The Court also observed that different Judges may legitimately take a different view of what is "just and equitable" in particular circumstances.

The Court in this case reduced the appellate court's finding of contributory negligence at 70% to 50%. The trial judge had found that the pursuer was 90% contributorily negligent.

The case just goes to show how difficult it can be to assess contributory negligence.

I suggest that all that a competent catastrophic injury lawyer can do is to try and extract general principles from the cases and apply them to the facts. It is best to avoid trying to find "comparable" cases because no two cases are the same and reported cases do not contain the case papers and photographs of the scene of the accident. Lawyers and Judges will of course vary in their approach to contributory negligence.

As Baroness Hale once observed at the Personal Injury Bar Association conference 2019: –

> "***The Supreme Court is not the final Court because it is always right; it is right because it is the final Court***".

Liability and contributory negligence, particularly in respect of pedestrian liability is one example where that statement is exactly on point.

Approval of liability

Any settlement on the issue of liability where the Claimant lacks capacity will of course need the approval of the Court in order for it to be binding upon the parties. It is usual to therefore conclude the issue of liability with an approval hearing upon this issue prior to proceeding to directions in relation to quantum.

Appropriate consideration should also be given to anonymity in a catastrophic case right at the commencement of the case. In proceedings in the High Court in London, the pleadings can be discovered online by the press and public who may run a story on the matter now well before any hearing.

Conclusion and practice points

I have tried to extract some of the principles in the case law involving pedestrians.

- Catastrophic brain injury lawyers frequently have to grapple with such issues and they are made all the more difficult by the potential inability of the Claimant to give evidence in the case or else remember what happened.

- If you apply the principles set out here, they will help but such cases are risky for both sides. Settlement of such issues is always a wise course if possible.

- Is this a case where a reasonably competent driver should have predicted the sudden movement of the pedestrian in front of the car. That is the key question.

- Should the Defendant have been on notice of a “real risk” as opposed to a mere possibility that the pedestrian would emerge suddenly into the path of the car.

- Needless to say it is vital to take the appropriate advice from experienced Counsel as soon as possible, that means as soon as you get the case, not a year down the line or more, and to maintain the appropriate advice through to settlement or trial.

- You and Counsel will need to consider whether expert evidence is necessary and how that expert evidence should be obtained.

- It is imperative that primary evidence such as vehicles, and CCTV should be preserved.

CHAPTER EIGHT

STARTING AND MANAGING THE CLAIM

We turn to the steps necessary to intimate the claim and the evidence that will be reasonably required to resolve the proceedings.

This may, in a catastrophic case be resolved at more than one, perhaps numerous CCMC's or not at all by a Court and consensually if there is no pressing need to issue proceedings.

In many catastrophic brain injury cases of course, time will never begin to run, provided that since the accident the Claimant has never regained capacity.

However, if there could be any doubt about capacity it is always wisest to issue well within the 3-year limitation period or seek a clear written agreement for an extension of the limitation period from the Defendant(s) unequivocally. In many cases however you will need to seek an approval of a liability apportionment either by way of Part 7 or Part 8 proceedings. If under Part 7, the case can then be stayed.

Detailed letter of claim

The starting point will be an early notification letter of claim to the insurance company and setting out the nature of the catastrophic injury and that it be placed with the appropriate team and that it falls outside a protocol. The letter of claim in such a case needs to be well constructed. It is used by the insurer to

1. Determine the category of team that will take the case on

2. The potential reserve.

If you are at all unsure, seek Counsel's advice even before you draft the letter of claim.

Many serious/catastrophic fee earners now have back door channels and good relationships with named contacts at insurers and you should check with your senior partners/director as to the appropriate person to be put in touch with if you do not have such a contact.

One law firm, hold an annual dinner every year to which they invite Defendant Solicitors and Insurers to celebrate the collaborative relationship that they have with them! What a brilliant idea.

It's always worth picking up the phone with such a contact when you have one. Nothing fosters collaborative working better than being open and informative where possible and communication in person or by video or telephone is better than "keyboard warrior" emails. Letting somebody know what is coming is just common professional courtesy.

Application of the Serious Injury Code and whether the insurer is a party or will agree to abide by the Code should be considered initially. The problem with the code is that it is not universally adopted and it is also unenforceable.

Some firms now enter into written agreements about what is expected conduct wise from each side, consensually with extensions of limitation, timetabling and exchange of evidence built in without the need to trouble the Court. There are sanctions built in sometimes to the agreement for failure to abide by them.

Early interim payments

Even where liability remains not admitted, in many cases, the "writing is on the wall" for primary liability at least, and the Defendant should and will often co-operate with providing sometimes significant interim payments particularly if the Claimant's team is going to be open with disclosure and access to medical experts to examine the Claimant.

Be realistic with requests however particularly where liability is going to be an issue. The Claimant will either be in hospital or in a rehabilitation centre funded by the NHS or the Integrated Care Board (ICB). Interim payments should initially be directed towards the instruction of a good "BABICM" registered Brain Injury Case Manager preferably on a unilateral basis and the preparation of an Initial Needs Assessment (INA). The British Association of Brain Injury and Complex Case Management (BABICM) keep a list of their members on their website and is accessible here.

https://www.babicm.org/

Statutory Funding and Care

A large book could be written on statutory funding alone. It is a very specialist area. In short, there is

1. Health care funding

2. Social care funding.

NHS funding and Integrated Care Board Funding for catastrophically injured claimants are health care funding.

The principal statute is the Care Act 2014 but it has been amended significantly. There is a nice lay summary of the Act on the Carers UK website.

https://www.carersuk.org/help-and-advice/guides-and-tools/your-guide-to-the-care-act-england/

NHS England is responsible for commissioning primary care services. The Health and Care Act 2022 enables the NHS to delegate to an ICB (from 1st July 2022) any or all of its statutory functions for directly commissioning healthcare services and paying providers for them. A delegation agreement will be put in place between the ICB and NHS England. ICB's have replaced Clinical Commissioning Groups (CCG's).

ICBs have their own leadership teams, which include a chair and chief executive, and also include members from NHS trusts/foundation trusts, local authorities, general practice, and an individual with expertise and knowledge of mental illness.

An integrated care system (or ICS) is a partnership of organisations that come together to plan and deliver joined up health and care services, and to improve the lives of people who live and work in their area.

Following several years of locally-led development, recommendations of NHS England and Royal Assent of the Health and Care Act (2022), 42 ICSs were established across England on a statutory basis on 1 July 2022

Each ICS will include an integrated care board (as described above) and also an integrated care partnership (as described below).

An integrated care partnership (or ICP) is a statutory committee jointly formed between the NHS integrated care board and all upper-tier local authorities that fall within the ICS area. The ICP will bring together a broad alliance of partners concerned with improving the care, health and wellbeing of the population, with membership determined locally. The ICP is responsible for producing an integrated care strategy on how to meet the health and wellbeing needs of the population in the ICS area.

In many cases, as the Claimant recovers from the severe traumatic brain injury, there may come a point where primary health care needs effectively cease and this becomes a case for social care. In that case Social Care Funding from the local authority will become more relevant.

Statutory funding is going to be essential to investigate particularly where liability is in dispute and a finding of contributory negligence is a possibility or where liability has been settled with a deduction.

This is likely to become very relevant as the Claimant steps down from hospital care to secondary care facilities for the purposes of specialist brain injury rehabilitation and hopefully then home to new or adapted accommodation with a dedicated care and therapy team at home.

Investigation of statutory funding is going to be required and you may wish to enlist the help of a statutory funding expert to advise at an early juncture.

Often this can be done on a joint basis with the Defendant as the interest is common to ensure that state funding is maximised.

Care claims and the risk of double recovery.

A common scenario is where the Claimant has significant care needs currently being met by the state but he includes a claim for a private care regime which he intends to set up. What is to stop the Claimant from claiming private care and then utilising state funded care. This was considered in *Peters v East Midlands Strategic Health Authority*_[2010] QB 48, and [2009] EWCA Civ 145.

These are the principles:-

1. The Claimant who wishes to opt for private care in preference to statutorily funded care is entitled to do so as a matter of right.

2. There cannot be double recovery however.

3. A promise by the Deputy to the Court not to apply for state funding is unlikely to be accepted as circumstances can change and another Deputy could not be bound by the promise.

4. In the Court of Appeal, another solution was found called a "Peters Promise". That is a promise that if the Claimant receives state funding in the future, he will indemnify the Defendant to the extent of the funding that he receives.

My own experience and that of others is that such promises are very rarely sought as they are virtually impossible to police. With the greater difficulty in obtaining state funding and the difficult state that public services currently find themselves in, the provision of high quality publicly funded care is becoming rather more difficult to achieve.

My view on Peters

I have never understood the Peters decision. In reality, the Court was overly concerned by the prospect of "double recovery".

1. There was no prospect of the Claimant obtaining the same damages twice over from the Defendant. It is difficult to see therefore why this was termed double recovery. The Defendant would pay care damages that were owed. The Claimant may instead receive a "windfall" not double recovery if the Claimant utilised statutory funding instead.

2. Claimant's receive windfalls all the time and it is no concern of the Courts. A Claimant who successfully believes he will utilise

private surgery and recovers the costs but 10 years later genuinely changes his mind and uses the NHS has received a windfall.

3. A Claimant who recovers care costs but makes do with less receives a "windfall".

4. A Claimant who has insurance they have paid for to cover a loss is able to nevertheless recover the loss from the Defendant. Courts don't worry about double-recovery in that situation.

5. Courts make findings of fact about future events either on a probability or on a percentage chance basis (see Davies v Taylor in the House of Lords if you don't accept that). Take future private versus NHS surgery costs as an example. The Court must make findings of fact at trial which may range from:-

    a. The Claimant will undergo private surgery;

    b. The Claimant will probably undergo private surgery

    c. There is a chance the Claimant may or may not undergo private surgery.

    d. The Claimant will probably utilise the NHS.

    e. The Claimant will definitely utilise the NHS.

Once the finding of fact has been made, the Court does not then worry about double recovery. If the finding is that the Claimant will undergo private surgery, and gets paid for that surgery in full, nobody goes back to recoup that cost of surgery if the Claimant in fact does not utilise that money for private surgery. Nobody has to give an undertaking or a promise. The Claimant after the award has been made is entitled to use that award as they wish.

Peters was a difficult decision to understand. It is no surprise then that Peters is perhaps falling into obscurity and rightly so, it is submitted.

Local authority cannot take the damages award into account

A local authority will be acting unlawfully if it takes into account a damages award and decides for that reason under a means test to refuse statutorily funded care. The relevant decision is *Tinsley v Manchester City Council & South Manchester CCG* [2017] EWCA Civ 1704.

Section 117 of the Mental Health Act 1983- There is no allowance under Section 117 for making a financial charge for services, residential or non-residential.

Personal injury awards administered by the Court of Protection are specifically excluded from calculations of capital, generally the local authority are not entitled to take such damages into account. However the Health and Care Act 2022 has reduced protection to people with assets where the above does not apply.

This is however beyond the scope of the book. Specific advice should be sought in this area from a statutory funding expert or lawyer specialising in this field.

Care before the accident

Where the Claimant already needed some care before the accident, practitioners should consider the case of *Martin v Salford Royal NHS Foundation Trust* [2021] EWHC 3058. HHJ Bird awarded the full cost of private care not just the additional care needed as a result of the accident.

The position is even more difficult with a periodical payments order (PPO). Most payments for future care in catastrophic cases will be under a PPO except where there is contributory negligence and the Claimant may be advised to seek a lump sum award or where there are other considerable risks in the case.

The Judge cannot therefore reduce the multiplier in a PPO case to reflect the risk of double recovery. The reality is that the system is beginning to accept the possibility of the claimant being placed in the position being able to recover both his damages and statutory funding. This is the problem with a once and for all system. In reality at a trial there would be a finding of fact as to whether the Claimant will utilise statutory care or a private regime (reflecting the chances of each perhaps) and that will determine the extent of the award.

Managing the family's expectations

Even the most experienced Leading Counsel, Senior Juniors and Senior Partners can find this challenging. A family is torn apart by a catastrophic injury and pre-existing issues or divisions can be exacerbated. A large part of your time will be spent managing and helping the family who will essentially need to be guided not only through the litigation process but the rehabilitative process all whilst grieving for the relative or partner they have nearly lost.

The litigation friend will be giving instructions in the case but this doesn't mean that welfare decisions should not involve all relevant parties. The litigation friend must act in the Claimant's best interests or they can be removed and replaced.

Sometimes there is no appropriate or any litigation friend and I have had cases where the appointed firm of deputies have also acted as litigation friend. They are frequently extremely helpful and if it is approached in the right way, costs of instructing a professional litigation friend may still may be recoverable.

There can be issues between spouse and parents, former partners who for example may claim the breakup was temporary and brothers, sisters, step-brothers and so on. Modern families are complicated and so will be the litigation process.

The issue of where the Claimant is to be transferred for slow-stream rehabilitation will often be contentious and there may be no agreement. Clinical treating team and the family may also conflict.

An experienced brain injury specialist, Senior Junior and Leader will have experienced many of the issues before and will be useful from an early stage to guide you and the family through these issues as will an experienced brain injury case manager.

Quite often family therapy and psychological treatment for traumatised parents or a spouse will also be required and should be considered by way of funding from the Defendant or by interim payment.

Investigation reports

There is an increasing difficulty in obtaining police reports or HSE or other investigatory reports where the Defendant is charged with an offence in the Crown Court. This is largely due to the fact that a trial can take months or even years to be reached and the trial process cannot be prejudiced by public disclosure of the documents. See *Conway v Rimmer* [1968] AC 910, (not a road traffic case however).

You will need to consider the ability to obtain disclosure. You cannot obtain third party disclosure without issuing proceedings in order to obtain disclosure against a third party such as the Police.

A pre-action disclosure application against a Defendant themselves may not be successful. To be in physical possession of say the police evidence for the purposes of the criminal proceedings, does not mean that legally the Claimant has possession or control. They may not be in possession of the documents for the purposes of disclosure because they do not have control of the documents. See for example, the decision of Master Brown in *Collette Turner v Sheffield Teaching Hospitals NHS Foundation Trust and the Healthcare Safety Investigation Board (Third Party)* [2023] EWHC 3452.

A Defendant may be forbidden from releasing the documents for any other purpose so it will be necessary to have a third-party disclosure application say against the Chief Constable of the Police Force.

There is guidance for the disclosure of material to third parties created by the Crown Prosecution Service. A link can be found here (at the time of writing) but a search should reveal the latest link.

https://www.cps.gov.uk/legal-guidance/disclosure-material-third-parties#:~:text=People%20who%20have%20made%20statements,would%20prejudice%20the%20criminal%20proceedings.

Here is a helpful extract from the key part of the guidance from the code. (Copyright belongs to the CPS).

> "Both the police and the CPS may be requested to disclose further material to those conducting civil proceedings, which would include a level of information in excess of the limited information anticipated by police guidance. This may include the witness statements and the analytical report produced by the Collision Investigator in a collision case involving injury or death.
>
> This guidance sets out how the disclosure of material on the police file should be made to the civil litigators.
>
> In all cases, the Police Collision Report, the Forensic Collision Investigators Report together with accompanying photographs, plans, CCTV footage and note book entries

> of reporting officers should be disclosed upon request. These may be edited before disclosure if necessary.
>
> In the majority of cases the police witness statements should also be disclosed providing permission has been given from the witness to disclose their statement. Bearing in mind the importance of the civil claim to the injured person and or dependents of the deceased, the police should encourage witnesses to assist in the civil claim where possible.
>
> In rare cases it is accepted that disclosure of the police witness statements may prejudice the criminal prosecution. In those cases, the police and the CPS must consider whether the police statement(s) can be disclosed or whether conditions need to be attached to disclosure (such as the timing of such disclosure). Whilst doing so, the reviewing lawyer must give consideration as to how any such conditions may affect the prosecutions obligations in respect of "unused material". Regard should also be had to the fact that if the civil litigator breaches imposed conditions they may face disciplinary proceedings by their professional body.
>
> If, after considering whether appropriate conditions can be attached to disclosure of police statements, the conclusion is that there is no workable solution and that significant risks would still remain, the police/CPS can refuse to disclose all or some of the police statements in the case. Again, it is repeated that this should only apply in rare circumstances."

I would recommend dealing with this in an early Consultation/ Conference.

Venue

Whilst the High Court in London, has traditionally been regarded as the only appropriate venue, and indeed still is where I probably conduct most of my cases.

Other High Court centres with an experienced Personal Injury Designated Civil Judge and team of good Personal Injury experienced District Judges should also be seriously considered. The senior judiciary are very keen to encourage catastrophic claims being issued outside London and in a liability case where witnesses would have to travel, Masters are increasingly prepared to transfer cases out to the District Registry whether you like it or not.

Manchester has a dedicated serious injury protocol and tailored directions under the leadership of His Honour Judge Nigel Bird.

Liverpool is able to deal with serious and catastrophic injury work under the leadership of His Honour Judge Graham Wood.

Leeds has a new recently Designated Civil Judge, His Honour Judge Mark Gargan.

CCMC

If the case is to be issued, we must remember that the case may also not be subject to a costs budget, if the case is highly likely to exceed £10 million (not unusual) or involves a child. The value and course that a catastrophic brain injury case may take is subject to change. In many cases a CMC will be listed rather than a CCMC. Check the order carefully as to what the Court has ordered. The Court may deal with budgeting later or not at all depending on the view they take of the case and the Defendant's attitude.

However, careful planning with Senior Counsel is essential prior to the CMC or CCMC and I would say months ahead of the time that directions, case summary and a budget (if needed) need to be filed.

However at a CCMC, the District Judge or Master will have to be satisfied that the expert evidence obtained is:-

a) Reasonably required to resolve the proceedings;

b) Needed to be instructed on a unilateral rather than joint basis;

c) Is proportionate in cost to the value in dispute, importance and complexity of the proceedings.

Necessity is trumped by proportionality and before embarking on multiple expensive evidence even in a catastrophic injury claim, we may need to consider budgets, the overall value of the claim and proportionality and to justify the instructions. The evidence required is likely to be all or some of the disciplines as follows:

- Liability – accident reconstruction and CCTV. If liability is in issue, you will be considering and probably asking for a "split trial".

- An Accident and Emergency Consultant, good for an overview and to signpost the evidence that will be required.

- A Consultant in Neuro-rehabilitation, probably your next go to report to comment on the severity of the TBI, causation and the rehabilitation process.

- Orthopaedic Surgeons- Ironically, in a catastrophic TBI claim, orthopaedic and spinal issues can be missed if you are not careful.

- General Surgery

- A Neuropsychologist
- A Neurosurgeon or Neurologist, (probably the latter) and not usually both but possibly;
- A Neuro-radiologist
- A Neuropsychiatrist
- Neuro-otology or ENT or both
- Neuro-ophthalmology
- Life Expectancy
- Speech and Language Therapy
- Physiotherapy
- Nursing Care
- Occupational Therapy
- Music Therapy
- Employment
- Assistive Technology
- Transportation
- Accommodation
- Financial advice on the form of award.

- And more…

Directions and hearings in the KB Division of the High Court, London

A collaborative and staged approach to the evidence would be sensible and advisable.

Most readers will be very familiar with litigating in the Royal Courts of Justice but it is always helpful to remind yourself and keep abreast of the latest guidance.

If litigating in the Royal Courts of Justice, the 10th edition of the King's Bench Guide (currently in force at the time of writing and just published on 19th April 2024) should be your veritable bible and is found online here:-

https://www.judiciary.uk/guidance-and-resources/kings-bench-guide-2024/

This tenth edition of the Guide makes some further changes since the full revision of the Guide in the 2022 edition. Those changes relate to:

- Updated guidance on open justice, anonymity and non-disclosure orders

- Updated guidance on contempt applications

- Updated guidance as to resources available to litigants in person

- Updated guidance on resources in respect of vulnerable witnesses.

- Updated notice of allocation

- Amendment to Masters' Hearing Directions
- KB Masters Clerks' contact detail

The most thumbed part is usually the Masters contact details and their clerks at pages 214-215 and 224-226.

At the time of writing the Masters in the High Court are:-

- Senior Master Cook
- Master Eastman
- Master Davison
- Master Thornett
- Master Gidden
- Master Sullivan
- Master Dagnall
- Master Stevens
- Master Armstrong
- Master Brown.

In order to obtain a Masters appointment as well as the usual application you will need to properly complete the Master's appointment form where the hearing is longer than 30 minutes. The form can be downloaded here:-

https://www.gov.uk/government/publications/kings-bench-masters-appointment-form

Incidentally, all Masters are now addressed as "Judge" in Court, not Sir or Madam (or as Master McCloud once told me, she was occasionally addressed as "Mistress" which didn't particularly impress her!). Master Eastman likes to be addressed still as "Master".

Anonymity Orders

See carefully the section on applications for anonymity at section 4.11 of the guide and note my guidance why an anonymity may need to be obtained at the outset of the commencement of proceedings not merely upon settlement or trial.

The Anonymity Order (February 2024 version, currently at the time of writing) is in draft and must comply with the technical requirements. It is found here:-

https://www.gov.uk/government/publications/form-pf10-anonymity-and-prohibition-of-publication-order.

CHAPTER NINE

REHABILITATION

The catastrophically brain injured client will often spend many weeks or months in hospital before being transferred to a residential rehabilitation unit.

The aim is to allow the Claimant ultimately to return to some form of living in the community usually with a considerable and very substantial support package.

However sometimes there are such severe behavioural problems that they cannot be managed in the community but that is very rare.

Living in the community however is associated with better outcomes for quality of life namely:-

1. Undertaking activities;

2. Increased independence gives better self-esteem and quality of life.

3. Contact with family and friends.

We have already touched upon statutory funding.

In the UK at least, the restriction on funds means that most Claimants will not receive sufficient input and this is a real source of anxiety and frustration to families of the brain injury Claimant and one as a legal practitioner in charge of the claim that you will have to manage. It creates a great pressure for progress and the need for substantial interim payments right from the outset.

In a case where liability is not admitted at the outset and this is increasingly common due to more criminal charges being heard in the Crown Court rather than the Magistrates' Court, there is often very little choice but to use the statutory therapies and care provided by the state. Physiotherapy and occupational therapy may be limited and there is often insufficient co-ordination of therapies when they are provided. Some institutions are better than others.

Your first step therefore even in a case where liability decisions have not been made, will usually be to request funding for an immediate needs assessment (INA) and for rehabilitation. The serious Injury guide agreed between APIL (Association of Personal Injury Lawyers) and FOIL (Forum of Insurance Lawyers) encourages this but as I have observed, lacks enforceability if the other party does not wish to abide by it.

If funding is provided, the Defendant will probably choose the Direct Funding method so that the Defendant essentially decides albeit hopefully in a collaborative way what will be funded and what will not be funded. This can be fine where the parties agree but if the contrary is true it is a source of real frustration to the family of the Claimant. The Claimant is not in a strong position to disagree before liability can be determined.

There are only 2 methods of funding by the Defendant.

1. Direct funding. The Defendant ultimately agrees or does not agree to fund particular therapies, support workers, and case management.

2. General Interim payments. The Claimant's team then identifies the needs but runs the risk ultimately as to whether they are recovered.

Case Management

The case of *Wright v Sullivan* [2005] EWCA Civ 656 is clear that the case manager owes a duty to the patient and no other person. Where option 2 is chosen, you will bear the responsibility of proving (along with the case manager) whether the care and treatment regime is reasonable and recoverable.

We have already referred to the case manager selection process. Not every case manager works well with each family type so you may have to have 3 or 4 selected and see which works best for the particular Claimant and family. A "beauty parade" means that the litigation friend and family are brought into the decision and more likely to be vested in the choice.

Transitional stages

These are:-

1. Hospital to rehabilitation or residential placement.

2. Residential rehabilitation to "slow-stream" (long-term) rehabilitation. This may occur many years after the traumatic brain injury and looks for small steady accumulation of gains over time.

3. Transfer to Neuro-behavioural units where severe neuro-behavioural problems can be managed.

4. Rehabilitation/residential placement/ slow-stream or neuro-behavioural unit to home (community). Most brain injury survivors are cared for in the community but some will not be.

5. From living with family to supported/independent living. For some but not all.

Generally, the more severe the consequences of the brain injury the less likely each subsequent transitional stage is likely to occur. Of course, stages may be missed out and leap-frogged as well.

In the transitional stages, the Claimant may at first go home for weekends for example giving a useful insight and graded introduction to the next stage of rehabilitation. There may be an independent supported living trial in community style apartments within the grounds of the rehabilitation unit such at "TRU".

Therapists

The following therapists may well be involved in rehabilitating the Claimant.

- Neuropsychologist
- Consultant in neuro-rehabilitation
- Neuropsychiatrist
- Occupational Therapist
- Neuro-physiotherapist
- Speech and Language therapists
- Music therapists
- Art therapists
- Educational psychologist
- Sensory integration OT's

It is important however not to overload catastrophically brain injured patients or introduce too many therapists or to introduce them all too quickly.

Families may need help in understanding that not too much can be done all at once because of the likelihood of exhausting the Claimant and it being counter-productive.

Understandably families may expect that "more is better" when in fact this is unlikely to be the case especially in the early stages. The brain injured Claimant needs time to rest, sleep and recover and the decisions of the treating clinicians almost inevitably need to be respected.

The care package

Nursing care and support workers can supplement the care provided in a rehabilitation centre where this is permitted. It can however be trickier than you think to supplement care due to the statutory funding rules and/or the rules of the rehabilitation unit. NHS funding or "healthcare funding" does not allow top-up care but Social Care funding does allow top-up care and therapies. Much of your time will be spent trying to resolve these issues.

The aim is to recruit nursing care or support workers to meet the Claimant's reasonable needs in the community once they leave residential rehabilitation.

The care can either be provided by:-

1. Direct Recruitment
2. Agencies.

Both have their advantages and disadvantages but for long-term care and support and to work with a family in the long-term, direct recruitment is likely to be preferable.

Sometimes behaviour is so challenging that agency provision is the only option because of the difficulty of obtaining support workers who will bear the burden for any length of time.

Conversely, in complex brain injury there is an argument that specialist direct recruitment is the only answer to the complexity of the problems faced.

Neuropsychology

A treating neuropsychologist is going to be an essential element of the rehabilitation process. In conjunction with the neuro-rehabilitation consultant, they will devise a programme of rehabilitation for the Claimant. The aim is to support the Claimant to reach the maximum possible functioning and quality of life and to support the Claimant's family.

Reports

In order to co-ordinate the treatment programme there will be regular reports from all the therapists and case manager. There will be support worker notes. All of these become disclosable and part of the Claimant's treatment notes. They must be carefully managed and disclosed on a rolling basis to the Defendant. If any privileged conversations in the true sense of legal privilege find themselves into these notes (which they should not) then these will need editing before disclosure.

I would say that these documents are fundamental to the medico-legal opinions that will follow.

Medico-legal experts will see this considerable volume of documents and opine accordingly on what they read and lawyers must therefore read and understand them too.

The documents in such cases frequently are over 10,000 pages of evidence. (A lever arch file contains about 300-400 pages).

Careful pagination, and fact management are essential. It is no surprise therefore that true catastrophic injury lawyers may have no more than 10 ongoing cases at any one time. It takes time to truly prepare a catastrophic brain injury claim particularly as the effects of traumatic brain injury cannot be assumed, or pigeon-holed. Every brain injury is truly unique.

Legal costs of attending rehabilitation meetings

In *Hadley v Pryzybylo* [2024] EWCA Civ 250 the Court of Appeal held that the costs of attending rehabilitation case management meetings and other like meetings were recoverable as costs as Section 51(1) of the Senior Courts Act 1981 provides for a party to recover the costs incidental to the proceedings. The criteria are:

1. Utility

2. Relevance

3. Attributability

Costs which meet the above criteria and are reasonable and proportionate ought to be recoverable and ought to be included in any costs budget. Beware however, routine attendances not necessary will not probably be recoverable.

Accommodation

If a return to the home is to be made, it is almost an inevitability that new accommodation will need to be sourced usually on a single-storey level for the Claimant and his team of carers, and therapists. You will need to seriously consider at what stage a significant interim payment to purchase the accommodation can be secured either by consent or by application to the Court. Alternatively, is the Claimant to rent the accommodation until that can be obtained?

There will be practical difficulties around securing such accommodation and it takes around 6 months to a year as a rule of thumb to adapt accommodation. There will need to be sufficient space for the care and therapy team and the family who are to live with the Claimant.

Clearly, these issues will need careful and early consideration in a conference/Consultation with Counsel and Leading Counsel and cannot be left until the stage that the Claimant is to be discharged into the community.

Practice Points

- An early conference with experienced brain injury Counsel is almost always indicated. Early instruction is to be preferred.
- Instruct a good BABICIM Case Manager appropriate to this Claimant and this family. Your "usual" choice may not be right. Consider at least 3 different case managers.
- Make a case plan. Be prepared to update it regularly.
- Often you will have little choice but to appoint a case manager jointly. Remember not everything is perfect and something is better than nothing.
- Involve the family in the decision-making process of the appointment of a case manager. Remember it is they who will be working with the case manager more than you.

- You need to consider an INA usually at stage 2 of the process as the Claimant is transferred to in-patient rehabilitation.

- There are 2 methods of funding, Direct Funding from the Defendant or General Interim Payment. Both have advantages and disadvantages. You may not have much choice in the early stages.

- Plan ahead. Don't wait until it is too late. Time is never on your side in such cases.

- You may need these days to consider third party disclosure applications for police reports and such like. Delays in the system and new road traffic offences which are triable in the Crown Court mean that there are no often contested trials and delays. Careful advice is necessary.

- Commence your application for Deputyship early. There are delays in the Court of Protection and interim payments will need to be managed. See the next Section on Mental Capacity for further information on the tests.

CHAPTER TEN

MENTAL CAPACITY

We are concerned with Mental Capacity to Litigate and secondly Capacity to handle property and affairs. Capacity is governed now by the Mental Capacity Act 2005.

- "**Capacity**" is the ability to understand, retain and use information to make a decision, and to communicate any decision made.

- Capacity is **time and decision specific**, which means that every decision needs to be considered separately at the time the decision is required.

- Some people have capacity for some decisions but not for others, **this can change over time** and is **never diagnosis specific**.

- People's capacity **can fluctuate** and can be **impaired by many things** other than just brain injury, including various mental and other physical health conditions, ***emotional distress***, pain and substances such as alcohol, prescribed and non-prescribed drugs.

Section 2(1) of the Act which offers a definition of Capacity.

> "*For the purposes of this Act, a person lacks capacity in relation to a matter if at the material time he is unable to make a decision for himself in relation to the matter because of an impairment of, or a disturbance in the functioning of, the mind or brain*".

This is often referred to as "**the diagnostic threshold**". It is clear that psychiatric illness as well as organic brain injury fall within the definition.

It may be temporary or permanent

Why it matters?

Firstly, the Claimant's Solicitor is under a positive duty to be aware of and have proper regard to the client's mental Capacity:-

> ***"in taking instructions and during the course of the retainer, having proper regard to your client's mental capacity or other vulnerability, such as incapacity or duress;" Rule 1.6 of the Solicitor Rules SRA code of Conduct.***

Secondly, Part 21.1(2)(d) of the Civil Procedure Rules defines a "protected party" as a party or an intended party who lacks capacity to conduct proceedings. It also defines a "protected beneficiary" as a protected party who lacks capacity to manage and control any money recovered by or on their behalf or for their benefit in the proceedings.

- Rule 21.1(2)(c) adopts the definition as contained in the 2005 Act.

- CPR 21.2 requires a protected party to have a litigation friend to conduct the proceedings on their behalf.

- CPR 21.3(4) states that any step taken before a protected party has a litigation friend has no effect unless the court orders otherwise.

Thirdly, any settlement reached in respect of a person who later is found to lack mental capacity will not be binding on the Claimant unless approved by the Court.

- Therefore there is every reason for the Defendant to be interested in having a settlement approved by the Court where it has been alleged that the Claimant lacks mental capacity.

Fourthly, if the loss of capacity is permanent, the Claimant will wish to claim very substantial costs within the litigation of:-

- Deputyship, the appointment of a solicitor under the rules of the Court of Protection who will administer the proceeds of the litigation for the Claimant for life;

- The cost of statutory wills;

- The cost of applications to the Court of Protection during the course of the Claimant's lifetime.

The Mental Capacity Act has five principles:

1. **Assume capacity** – All adults are assumed to have sufficient capacity to make decisions, unless there is definitive evidence this is not the case.

2. **Support the individual**- Individuals must be helped to make their own decisions as far as practicable. It is important to be flexible and creative with communication and to give people time.

3. **Unwise decisions** – If someone makes a decision that other people would consider to be irrational, it does not mean they lack capacity, as long as they understand the reality of their situation.

4. **Best interests**- All decisions and actions must be taken in the best interests of the person lacking capacity.

5. **Least restrictive option**- All decisions and actions must be the least restrictive of the person's rights and freedom of action.

Burden of proof

Masterman-Lister v Brutton [2002] EWCA Civ 1889

Is on the person asserting incapacity i.e. The Claimant:

> ***"It is common ground that all adults must be presumed to be competent to manage their property and affairs until the contrary is proved, and that the burden of proof rests on those asserting incapacity".***

Section 1 of the Act provides for the following principles.

1. A person is assumed to have capacity unless it is established that he lacks capacity.

2. A person is not to be treated as unable to make a decision unless all practicable steps to help him to do so have been taken without success.

3. A person is not to be treated as unable to make a decision merely because he makes an unwise decision.

4. An act done or decision made for on behalf of a person who lacks capacity must be done, or made, in his best interests.

5. Before the act is done or decision made, regard must be had to whether the purpose for which it is needed can be as effectively achieved in a way that is less restrictive of the person's rights and freedoms of action.

Section 2 of the Act provides that:-

1. There must be an impairment of or disturbance of functioning of the mind or brain.

2. It can be permanent or temporary.

3. It cannot be established merely by appearance or age, a condition or aspect of behaviour which might lead others to make unjustified assumptions about his capacity.

4. It is a decision on the balance of probabilities.

Capacity is both **time and decision specific.**

A catastrophically brain injured will usually lack both litigation capacity and capacity to handle the proceeds of litigation permanently but some may regain some capacity at some stage. It therefore needs to be kept under careful review and cannot be assumed.

The following facts are relevant under section 3 of the Act in relation to ability to make decisions :-

1. Understanding of relevant information

2. Retaining that information

3. Using or weighing that information as part of the process of making the decision

4. Communicating that decision.

Explanations must be appropriate to his circumstances.

Information relevant to the decision includes the reasonably foreseeable consequences of deciding one way or another or failing to make the decision.

Application to the COP

The application to the Court of Protection involves the completion of the COP 1 Form in which a section must be completed by the relevant medical practitioner.

The guidance and forms are set out here.

https://www.gov.uk/government/collections/court-of-protection-forms

It would be usual to obtain advice from the proposed Deputy and instruct them to make the relevant application to the Court of Protection to appoint a Deputy.

Instructing the Neuro-psychiatrist

In relation to each category of cases, it is suggested that experts, usually the psychiatrist or neuro-psychiatrist, should be specifically directed to consider the following issues specifically.

Capacity to litigate.

The leading case is *Bailey v Warren* [2006] EWCA Civ 51. Lady Justice Arden (as she then was) provided a summary of matters which need to be considered when assessing whether a person has litigation capacity. These can be summarised as follows:-

- The nature of the proceedings;
- How the proceedings are being funded;
- The chances of the case not succeeding and adverse costs orders;

- The sorts of decisions that are likely to arise in the litigation. Has the Claimant's Solicitor given some examples of decisions likely to arise?

- Whether the Claimant has capacity to give proper instructions for and to approve the particulars of claim and schedule of loss and to approve a compromise;- Who signed the original documents or CFA?

- Whether the Claimant has an insight into the compromise, an ability to instruct his solicitors to advise him;

- Whether the Claimant has an ability to understand their advice and weigh their advice;

- Whether the Claimant would know what he was giving up and what would happen if he refused to accept an offer of compromise.

See also:

MacDonald J in *TB v KB and LH* [2019] EWCOP 14.

Property and affairs

- The value of the person's income and capital;

- Financial needs and responsibilities;

- Whether there are likely to be any changes in the person's financial circumstances in the foreseeable future;

- The skill, specialised knowledge and time it takes to manage the affairs properly;

- Whether a mental disorder is affecting the management of the assets; and

- Whether the person would be likely to seek, understand and act upon appropriate advice where needed in view of the complexity of the affairs.

- *Personal information*

- Age;

- Life expectancy;

- Psychiatric history;

- If so whether their welfare could be compromised;

- Prospects of recovery or deterioration;

- The extent to which the incapacity could fluctuate;

- The condition in which the person lives;

- Family background;

- Family and social responsibilities;

- The degree of support from others;

Vulnerability;

The following may also be relevant:-

- Whether the person could make rash or irresponsible decisions;

- Whether there could be exploitation by others. The family situation may be relevant;
- Whether other people's welfare are dependent upon the person.

How do Clinicians assess capacity?

It is multi-factorial. The following are relevant considerations:-

- Cognition;
- Non-cognitive neuropsychiatric factors:-
    - Impulsivity;
    - Motivation;
    - Apathy;
    - Psychomotor agitation;
    - Conduct disorder;
    - Personality disorder;
    - Drug and alcohol use;
    - Bipolar affective disorder;
    - ADHD;
    - Personality traits;
- Pre-injury ability;

- Insight;
  - Awareness of deficits;
  - Awareness of the effect of the deficits on person;
  - Awareness of deficits on self in society;
  - Insight is a scale but capacity is all or nothing;

Further reading on capacity assessments is available from the British Psychological Society "What makes a good assessment of Capacity".

See also:-

- Mental Capacity Act 2005

  http://www.legislation.gov.uk/ukpga/2005/9/pdfs/ukpga_20050009_en.pdf

- Mental Capacity Act 2005 Code of Practice

  https://www.gov.uk/government/uploads/system/uploads/attachment_data/file/497253/Mental-capacity-act-code-of-practice.pdf

- Law Society – Search "vulnerable clients"

Practice points

- Instruct a Neuro-Psychiatrist to deal with Capacity early. Never mind how bad the brain injury, it can never be assumed that a person has incapacity. It may not be contested but it needs evidencing.

- Prepare a detailed letter of instructing embodying the above principles.

- Instruct the proposed Deputy to make the application to the Court of Protection.

- Keep capacity under review.

CHAPTER ELEVEN

LATE COMPLICATIONS OF BRAIN INJURY

In severe traumatic brain injury there are the potentials for delayed complications and late complications. These are potentially:-

1. Hydrocephalus
2. Post-traumatic epilepsy
3. Alzheimer's disease
4. Hypopituitarism
5. Movement disorders
6. Parkinson's Disease
7. Kinetic tremors and dystonia

Hydrocephalus

This is marked by progressive mental deterioration. It is caused by an enlargement of the cavities deep within the brain called the ventricles which contain the cerebrospinal fluid. It is caused by disruption of the CSF absorption causing steady accumulation. Headaches worsen and the patient becomes confused, weak and unable to take part in rehabilitation. Treatment is usually by way of a ventriculo-peritoneal shunt or VP shunt. It is a problem for the medics rather than the lawyers.

Post traumatic epilepsy

This is an attack of altered consciousness due to disturbed electrical activity in the brain. There must be more than one episode of an attack in order to constitute a condition. It must be distinguished from faints.

Epilepsy gives rise to fits or seizures but the Claimant will be as usual in between the attacks. They can be major or minor, major ones resulting in loss of consciousness. Staring into space can mean a minor attack is taking place. A focal fit is where twitching occurs in a limb, which then progresses up the limb.

Complex partial seizures can be a combination of various sensations including altered sense of smell, taste, twitching and fidgeting.

Major seizures tend to cause loss of consciousness, stiffening and jerking of limbs. These are called tonic/clonic seizures. The Claimant will feel very tired for many hours afterwards.

Many of these events will occur soon in the immediate aftermath of the accident. However if they continue, seizures for example in the first week after the accident may predict the later onset of epilepsy.

Epilepsy is not unique to brain injury of course.

Epilepsy affects 1% of the population by age 20 and 3% of the population by age 75.

It affects around 1 in 100 people in the general population.

The long-term risk of developing epilepsy is called the LR or lifetime risk.

Lifetime risk in the population	
To age 50	1.6%
To age 80	3.0 %

Risk of early seizure with severe traumatic brain injury ranges from 14% to 30%.

The study by Annegers et al in 1998 defines as severe brain injury as loss of consciousness or amnesia for more than 24 hours, subdural haematoma or a brain contusion.

The standardised incidence ratio of developing epilepsy after a severe brain injury was 17 (95% confidence interval 12.3-23.6)

The significant risk factors for later seizures were:-

1. Brain contusion with sub-dural haematoma
2. Skull fracture
3. Loss of consciousness
4. Amnesia of more than one day
5. Age of 65 years or older.

80% of patients who will develop PTE will do so within 2 years of the accident.

94% of patients who will do so will develop it within 5 years of the accident.

The study by Fordington and Manford in 2020 shows that the presence of intra-cranial blood is the most important risk factor.

The Annegers study, "A population based study of seizures after traumatic brain injuries". The New England Journal of Medicine, 1998; 338(1): 20-24 provides the following risks for epilepsy after severe traumatic brain injury. These figures do not take into account the lifetime risk without brain injury, that is to say the figures needs further adjustment.

Year one	47-66%
Year 2-4	8-11.5%
Years 5-9	6-8.5 %
Years 10 on	2%

The epilepsy if it occurs can usually but not always be controlled by a single drug. Anticonvulsant medication can control between 66% and 75% of patients. However, some who has epilepsy will not be allowed to drive for at least one year from the date of last seizure. Working with heavy machinery or at heights should be avoided at least during the same period and HGV and PSV drivers will lose their licences. Adverse effects from the medication are however very unlikely.

Provisional Damages

The development of epilepsy in a catastrophic brain injury case is ironically going to be of less significance than in mild-moderate or moderate-severe traumatic brain injury claim. After all, the Claimant is going to have a significant nursing care package, is unlikely to work in any event and it may be thought that the provisional damages which is a discretionary remedy is going to be unlikely to significantly impact on the damages.

There are 3 questions:-

1. Is there a chance of the Claimant developing some disease or deterioration in their physical or mental condition which is measurable and not fanciful.

2. Is it serious?

3. Should the Court go on to exercise its discretion to award provisional damages.

The Claimant bears the burden of proving on the balance of probabilities the claim. The percentage risk if measurable need not be high. 1% or more will usually suffice.

On discretion however in *Curi v Collina* [1998] EWCA CIv 1326, Roch LJ endorsed the approach in *Allot v Central Electricity Generating Board (19th December 1998, unreported)* that the Court should **not** be "**very enthusiastic**" save in the clearest case.

The event if it occurred must mean that the Claimant would be undercompensated.

Provisional damages is therefore awarded for the risk of the Claimant developing epilepsy. You will need clear evidence from your neurologist on this issue.

However not every case is settled on a provisional damages basis and not every severe traumatic brain injury Claimant obtains an award at trial.

If the case reaches trial at say year 9 after the injury, If the risk of epilepsy is 2% and the risk in the general population is 1%, then there is a 1% increased risk after year 9 for life. If the chance of control is say 75% within a year the Court may refuse damages on a discretionary basis.

All will depend on the circumstances of the case so clear tailored medical evidence and advice will be required in every case.

Upon settlement, most Defendants would resist provisional damages or a variable PPO preferring the certainty of a final order. Many claimants now do not seek a variable PPO as they can be varied downwards as well as up.

Dementia

This has caused a lot of furore culminating in the relatively recent decision in *Matheu v Hinds* [2022] EWHC 924 QB. The Claimant was aged 29 at the date of the accident and sustained serious brain injury when as a pedestrian he was struck by a moped driven by the First Defendant.

He had made a very good recovery from his injuries and had gone onto enjoy a successful artistic career. He continued to suffer from headaches, fatigue and cognitive issues he said. He claimed provisional damages for dementia and epilepsy. He secured provisional damages for the risk of epilepsy but failed to do so for the risk of dementia.

The Court held that the Claimant needed to prove on the balance of probabilities that there was more than a fanciful chance that the TBI would cause him dementia in the future. This required him to prove that a single TBI can cause dementia and that this risk applied to him. The Court said that the answer to this remained doubtful as a matter of science. The Judge held that an association between two things didn't mean that one thing had caused the other especially where there was no clear understanding of what the causative route may actually be.

In the future, PET scanning may provide more information on the cause of the dementia especially if it was associated with areas of damage in the brain injury.

Therefore post-TBI dementia did not represent "the clearest case" as envisaged in Allott or a clear and severable risk, "a clear cut event" or "clear cut identifiable threshold".

The Judge therefore would have also not exercised their discretion.

The paper by Lo Bue and Callum 2020, suggested that if someone was to develop a dementing illness then symptoms may appear 12-24 months earlier.

I therefore suggest that for now until new research is conducted, the best way one can deal with dementia risk is to seek an enhancement for the possibility of increased care costs perhaps 12-24 months' worth if appropriate. That said, in a truly catastrophic claim it may be that the difference in the care package is just not discernible.

Of course, you have to ask your expert but make sure they are fully briefed on the literature that the Court reviewed in the case. Is there anything new or better evidence. If you are going to run the argument afresh, I respectfully suggest that anybody who does so will need epidemiology evidence as well as neurologists to give evidence on the issues arising.

Parkinson's Disease

Many of the points also apply in relation to Parkinson's Disease and it is suggested that the prospect of provisional damages is highly unlikely.

Life Expectancy

It must also be remembered that in a catastrophic injury claim there will be real issues of life expectancy. It is to that topic that we now turn.

CHAPTER TWELVE

LIFE EXPECTANCY

The standard approach to the assessment of life expectancy in the UK Courts, and any associated calculations of future losses, is to simply to use multipliers selected from the Ogden Tables.

There is a general consensus in the medical profession that persons with severe traumatic brain injury have increased mortality compared to the general population. Mortality is highest during the first year.

Causes of death may be:-

- Aspiration;
- Choking;
- Pneumonia;
- Kidney and urinary complications;
- Respiratory complications;
- Cardiovascular disease and complications;
- Risk of suicide;
- Accidental injury;
- Increased susceptibility of aging.

Life expectancy evidence is based on the projected life expectation in years to come. The research evidence comes principally from Strauss, Shavelle and Brooks et al. The Brooks paper however, indicates that there have been no such improvements in the TBI population in the past two decades. This has been demonstrated both in the United TBI States Model Systems and the California TBI databases. 7,8. Hence (in contrast to the general population) there does not appear to be any historical basis for the assumption that TBI life expectancy will improve in future decades.

In all cases of severe traumatic brain injury it is going to be essential to have evidence from:-

1. Clinicians

2. Possibly, and only if the clinicians are unable to deal with this to conclusion from statisticians or actuaries as to the Claimant's average life expectancy but for the accident and as a result of it.

It is useful to be able to have some understanding however and ability to assess life expectancy even on a rough and ready basis for now. That way realistic assessments of offers and reserves may be able to be made.

The point to remember is that all the research was conducted in the USA. And for once, the UK leads the way over the USA in respect of life expectancy of its citizens whether brain injured or not.

So, all the US figures for life expectancy require an adjustment so that they can be related to a Claimant in the UK.

Here is a method therefore of providing a rough working estimate of life expectancy in severe TBI cases. You have to work out your Claimant's life expectancy (unimpaired) as if he lived in the USA first. Then look at the literature and work out his impaired life now after the TBI.

Then work out as a percentage reduction.

Then apply this to his UK life expectancy using the Ogden Tables.

A convenient online calculator for US life expectancy in the absence of actuarial evidence is useful to calculate life expectancy in the USA (search USA Life Expectancy Calculator and choose one).

It is necessary to then consider the 2007 paper from Shavelle et al (part i) and the up-to-date 2015 paper (Part ii) on life expectancy by Brooks et al.

Brook's paper is also very helpful and perhaps the most recent work on TBI life expectancy. CDDS cohort is relevant for individuals less than 16 years of age as TBIMS does have data for individuals in this category.

The 4 groups they have defined are-

(1) **Does not walk, fed by others;**

(2) **Does not walk, self-feeds;**

(3) **Some walking with a handheld device or unsteadily alone; and**

(4) **Walks well alone.**

Decide which group your Claimant falls into.

The four functional categories were chosen by the researchers because feeding and mobility are the strongest predictors of longevity. There is only data for under 17-year olds in the CDDS data.

In the following worked example you may wish to search for and read a copy of the following article :-

> *"Long term disability and Survival in Traumatic Brain Injury: Results from the National Institute on Disability and Rehabilitation Research Model Systems" Brooks, Strauss, Shavelle et al in the Archives of Physical Medicine and Rehabilitation".*

The figure for the Model Systems group is slightly higher than that for the California group. This may be because the Model Systems Walking Criterion is more stringent (it requires that the person walks well for a distance of at least 150 feet, whereas the California criterion is only 20 feet). A further reason is that persons in the California group had ongoing disabilities that qualified them for state services, which is not true of all persons in the Model Systems group. For example, 58% of persons in the Model Systems "walks well" group were considered capable of living completely independently and 41% were capable of competitive employment.

Problems with the paper

- Whether a particular individual can be properly classified within the group;
- Clinicians tend to have difficulty with this and may well need help;
- Is the person's condition typical within the group
- What are the co-morbidities;
- Ignores whether a good care package helps;
- These are average survival times not specific to the individual;

- These are for the USA. The UK has better average life expectancy than the USA so it is necessary to adjust the figures;

Take an example of a male aged 15, we will call him "B" interpolating who is fed by others, life expectancy is a further 25 years (to age 40) (48.92% of his US Life expectancy)

- Using Table 1 Column 0% Discount Rate (to get his true lie expectancy in years) B will live for a further 71.87 years so to age 86.87 years on average.

- If B is able to be classed as self-feeding then his life expectancy is:-

  - 86.87 x 48.92% = 42.5 years

  - would be to 42.5 years of age.

  - So in the USA he would live to age 40.

  - His Life Expectancy in the UK however is higher 42.5 years of age.

- Beware of clinical experts simply looking at the papers and opining upon life expectancy. Such experts who do not make the adjustments properly will under-estimate life expectancy.

There are further problems

- The walking feeding disability groups are very wide with a wide range of ability in them.

- There are no clear definitions of self-feeding within the paper which are apparent to me. They normally use the Functional Independence Measure to assess ability. We will assume that B the Claimant is at present "does not feed" but that he is likely to fall between the two groups.

- The standard approach adopted by the English Courts of mapping percentages of US period measures of longevity onto the UK cohort estimates found in the Ogden Tables should be considered.

- *Robshaw v United Lincolnshire Hospitals NHS Trust* [2015] EWHC 923 (QB) contains a discussion of this issue with the Judge also accepting the argument that favourable economics, i.e. the award of substantial damages, can in itself enhance life expectancy.

- If B fell into the category of does not walk and does not feed. His life expectation is probably likely to be nearer around 42.5 years of age.

- There is potential for improvement on life expectancy up to age 61 if B self-feeds but I have no definition of that within the research. There will be variability within the group.

The Law

- The principles that apply to an application for permission to adduce that evidence. They are neatly summarised by Master Davison (formerly of 12 King's Bench Walk), in the case of *Dodds v Arif* [2020] PIQR P1 (N.B. his judgment has been cited with approval in the High Court on a number of occasions since – see *Ellis v Kelly and Chaplin v Pistol*).

- Life expectancy is a medical or clinical issue. In practical terms Master Davison held that, it is more convenient and cost-effective to ask the clinical experts for their opinion on life expectancy. Even if recourse to statistics is required, then that material is still a matter for the clinicians in the first instance. It is only if they disagree on how to apply the statistics that a statistician or bespoke life expectancy expert might be required.

- Bespoke life expectancy evidence should be confined to cases where the clinical experts cannot offer an opinion at all, or where they have stated that they require specific input from a life expectancy expert.

Conclusions on life expectancy in severe traumatic brain injury

- There is likely to be considerable reduced life expectancy in Severe/catastrophic TBI cases.
- The key factors are mobility and ability to feed.
- People may fall between groups.
- It is for the lawyers, failing which, the statisticians to help the clinicians.
- The clinical view must come first.
- If the clinicians cannot opine or need help then actuarial evidence may be needed.

Practice Points

- It is vital to consider life expectancy in such cases and not wait until this is raised by the Defendant.

- Rehabilitation will provide the potential for improved life expectancy as well as quality of life with focus on ability to self-feed and walk.

- Good clinical and probably actuarial evidence (if permitted by the Court) will be needed in such cases prior to the preparation of the final schedule of loss prior to trial or settlement.

- A Periodical Payments Order (or Variable order?) is likely to be highly desirable but financial advice from the appropriate expert will be needed.

- It is important to recognise how life expectancy is calculated on US life expectancy. I have shown how a rough and ready adjustment can be made for UK Life Expectancy as many clinicians do not appreciate the importance of undertaking this exercise.

- It is worthwhile emphasising that, once bespoke life expectancy is found to be appropriate, it is open to claimants to advance evidence that, pre-accident, they had a greater life expectancy than the norm (whether due to good health, a low BMI, a lack of smoking, area of the country in which they resided or whatever) and for Defendant to advance evidence of lower than average life expectancy before the accident.

- There are different camps over whether life expectancy should be calculated on Tables 1 and 2 of the Ogden Tables or Tables 28/36. It makes less difference when the Discount Rate is set closer to zero. The Odgen Committee's view is that it should be Tables 1 and 2. This is probably the better view.

CHAPTER THIRTEEN

THE CARE REGIME

For a catastrophically injured brain injury victim, the long-term care requirements will usually be very obvious and there will be a need for a round-the-clock care team. Where the Claimant has made a good recovery from a very severe brain injury there may well be a continuing claim for support. Understanding the following terms may be helpful.

- "Team Leader" – A person who manages and co-ordinates the team of carers.
- "Carer" – a person who provides actual nursing care.
- "Support worker – A person who provides generic support but falling short of actual nursing care.
- "Buddy" – More like a paid "friend" helping to provide peer support who needs social and community support.
- "Personal assistant" (PA) – More like a supervisor to assist with high level tasks such as paying bills, paperwork and administrative organisation.

Care and case management is going to inevitably be the largest element of quantum in a catastrophic brain injury claim and also therefore where the greatest disputes occur.

In short, the purpose of care is to put the Claimant back into the position as if the accident had not happened in so far as that is possible. Reasonableness is the key point which can in my view be thought of in this way. If an injured person could afford to pay for the care themselves, what, acting sensibly, would they pay for?

More legalistically:-

- Is the provision chosen and claimed reasonable?
- If the provision claimed is reasonable, the Claimant need not go for the cheaper option even if that is reasonable too.
- The problems associated with severe traumatic brain injury are physical, cognitive and emotional. Even where there has been a good recovery and return to community living, the residual deficits are likely to be long-term and ongoing.
- Reliance on family care is not a good answer. Marital relationships have a high rate of breakdown post brain-injury.

Physical problems include:-

- Hemi-paresis- an inability to move or weakness on one side of the body (the left side of the brain controls the right side and vice-versa);
- Ataxia-a group of disorders involving poor muscle control that affect, co-ordination, balance and speech;
- Impaired balance;
- Visual problems or cortical blindness;
- Fatigue.

Cognitive problems include:-

- Impaired memory;
- Inability to concentrate;

- Inability to learn;
- Executive problems- an inability to plan, organise, problem solve and think;
- Speech and language impairments such as expressive or receptive dysphasia (partial loss of language) or aphasia (complete loss of language skills) or dysarthria (difficulty in speaking clearly and fluently).

Emotional problems include:-

- Impulsivity;
- Unrestrained behaviour;
- Disinhibition;
- Anger;
- Hostility;
- Personality change;
- Difficulty in initiation;
- Decreased motivation;
- Loss of sensitivity and emotion;
- Increase in emotion and distress;
- Anxiety.

Severe traumatic brain injury puts an enormous strain on the family yet some cultural nuances particularly in a few traditional Asian families can produce a reluctance to accept care.

Young adults who have recovered from a child brain injury are also sometimes reluctant to engage with support in their younger years. They frequently end up in aimless, chaotic existences, serial relationships and end up in trouble with the criminal justice system.

Assessment of care and support needs

The assessment of care and support needs post-severe or catastrophic brain injury is therefore a vastly complex and difficult assessment and there is frequent scope for disagreement between experts instructed on both sides.

The starting point when considering and choosing a care expert is their experience in traumatic brain injury. There are experts who essentially do practise only in TBI claims and they are likely to have a considerable advantage over generalists.

In most cases you will need a separate occupational therapist to report upon aids and equipment and rehabilitation potential for the future as well as a care expert.

A good care expert will think about the challenges for this particular claimant for the future.

As Lord Blackburn said in *Livingstone v Rawyards Coal Co* (1880) 5 App Cas 25, the purpose is to

> ***"to objectively assess what is that sum of money which will put the party who has been injured in the same position as he would have been in, if he had not sustained the wrong for which is now getting his compensation".***

Of more modern cases you will need to consider:-

CCC v Sheffield Teaching Hospitals NHS Foundation Trust [2023] EWHC 1770 KB. The following passage is very useful when considering the skills your care expert needs to bring to the case. Ritchie J said:-

> **"89. I found Miss Sargent's substantial experience in case** *management and in the construction implementation and management of care packages for cerebral palsy children impressive. Her reports were clear and succinct and her figures were based on real experience in the field. I consider that her estimate of the past care hours was realistic and deducted the care that M would have provided to an able-bodied child properly. I consider that Miss Sargent elucidated and clarified the key points relevant to the issues of past care and using Thornbury nurses during COVID, the past care rates for gratuitous care and her assessment of the Claimant's needs for future care were all reasonable, balanced and consistent. The main substantial defect in Miss Sargent's evidence was her error in drafting the first joint statement in relation to current and future night care needs."*

See also:-

- *Loughlin v Singh [2013] EWHC 1641*
- *Farrugia v Burtenshaw & MIB [2014] EWHC1036*
- *Tate v Ryder Holdings [2014] EWHCC 4256*
- *Whiten v St George's Healthcare NHS Trust [2011] EWHC 2066*
- *Ali v Caton & MIB [2013 EWHC 1730*

The following issues are often prevalent in catastrophic brain injury claims:

- The need for a second carer;
- The need for overnight support;
- The need for a waking night carer versus a sleep-in carer;
- The hours of support required during the day;
- Holiday needs;
- Need for aids and equipment;
- The level of need of case management;
- Needs for therapeutic intervention in the short and long-term.

The expert needs to deal properly with:-

- The importance of selecting the right candidates and the level of knowledge and training;
- The training and support that the carers and support workers will need;
- The need for double-up care where there are physical impairments affecting the ability to transfer independently and/or emotional deficits which could pose a serious risk of aggressive behaviour where the safety of one carer would be in doubt;

- The need for a second carer was discussed in the case of *Farrugia v Burtenshaw & MIB and Quinn Insurance Ltd* [2014] EWHC 1036.

Practice points

- This is likely to be the largest head of claim and where you will need to spend a lot of time and effort.
- The careful selection of your care expert is paramount. Seek Counsel's advice before instructing and have a number of conferences/consultations with the experts.
- The family and their expectations of being able to care for the Claimant are likely to need careful management.
- Establishing the care regime is likely to be very helpful in assessing what is needed.
- A good case manager must critically analyse the care package. Care experts and case managers should be alert to changing conditions, clinical and social needs and circumstances of the Claimant.
- With a dynamic and expert case manager and care expert, OT and rehabilitation team, catastrophically brain injured Claimants can reach their best potential, need lesser support and maximise their quality of life.

CHAPTER FOURTEEN

SETTLEMENT

The vast majority of catastrophic brain injury claims are settled at a joint settlement meeting or mediation before trial but this will not inevitably be so. Fail to prepare and prepare to fail and never assume that your case will settle. If you don't prepare for trial, it probably won't settle or not at the right value.

Inevitably, catastrophic brain injury claims will require the approval of the Court due to the fact that the Claimant will lack capacity.

See *Dunhill (a protected party by her litigation friend Tasker) v Burgin* [2014] All ER (D) 96 (Mar) [2014] UKSC 18.

Even if there is a risk that the Claimant lacks capacity, approval should be sought. See *Coles v Perfect* [2013] EWHC 1955 (QB). Note, only the High Court has this inherent jurisdiction, not the County Court, but no doubt you will have issued the case in the High Court in any event. It's also a good reason to resist a perhaps inexperienced managing Judge attempting to transfer your High Court matter to the County Court.

If legal proceedings were settled or compromised without it being recognised that one of the parties lacked that capacity so that she did not have the benefit of a litigation friend and the settlement was not approved by the court as also required by the CPR it will not be binding.

In *Dunhill* the fact that the settlement had been embodied in a consent order had not constituted the approval of the court for the purpose of CPR 21.10(1).

The purpose of that rule was to impose an external check on the propriety of the settlement and the accompanying practice direction set out the evidence which had to be placed before the court when approval was sought.

She ought to have had a litigation friend from the outset and any settlement should have been approved by the court under CPR 21.10(1). The consent order would be set aside and the case would go to trial.

Important points:-

1. Where capacity is doubted by either side on expert evidence, the claim will still need approval in order to ensure that it is binding.

2. Prepare a core bundle of documents for the Court. This will consist of the Pleadings, schedule and counter-schedules of loss, liability documents (if not already approved), Medical evidence for both sides, joint statements if any, and secondary reports in care and accommodation. Witness statements should be included but not the extensive medical and rehabilitation notes.

3. Remember to build in reading time into any time estimate for the Judge. They will thank you, don't rely on the Master or District Judge to remember to do this.

4. Draft orders most likely drafted by Counsel probably reflecting a periodical payments order for future care and case management but not inevitably so, will be present together with applications and draft order for an anonymity order if not already made.

5. Evidence on the form of award from a financial expert may need to be disclosed confidentially to the Judge or at least dealt with in Counsel's opinion.

6. Make sure that everything is <u>perfect</u> for the Judge. Bundles should be filed in time.

7. Try to have an interim payment on account of costs agreed and embodied in the order.

8. Ensure that the details for payment of the money are all in order and the Claimant's Deputy has provided this in writing.

9. Be prepared to have any deductions from damages approved by the Court.

10. Be prepared to have any claims for past care and distribution to the relatives, or carers embodied in the order.

11. Have the orders sent to Counsel in "Word" format so that the order can be perfected if needs be during the hearing.

12. There will need to be a confidential bundle consisting of Counsel's Opinion, and any unused medical evidence which is prepared for the Court's eyes only. If the bundle is an electronic one, please make sure that the physical and electronic page numbers match up. Also make sure that the index is hyperlinked and brings up the correct numbered page.

13. The issue of whether and what future losses are dealt with by a Periodical Payments Order and by way of lump sum has to be addressed in the confidential opinion or if a PPO was not agreed, why this was the case.

14. The Court will consider carefully the identity of the appointed Deputy at the hearing and will wish to ensure that there is no potential conflict. A recent decision has caused real difficulties

where an in-house Deputy has been appointed even where different alternatives were offered. I respectfully suggest it may be better to ensure independence and the Court's approval by seeking an independent Deputy to manage the funds. Firms can of course cross-sell to other personal injury firms so there is no need to be concerned.

15. Both Counsel/Leading Counsel, the Litigation Friend and Deputy along with one or two members of the close family will usually attend the hearing. The hearing is an important one emotionally as well as legally and can represent closure after many hard years for a Claimant and their family and possibly the only time they are present when their case has been heard in Court.

    Most Judges would recognise that and wish to have a word with the family. I recall His Honour Judge Gosnell in Leeds High Court would often step down from the bench to the floor of the Court to meet and greet the family (and Claimant if present), a very nice touch.

    It is I know, immensely satisfying for both Claimant and Defendant teams who have hopefully worked together collaboratively to see a catastrophically injured Claimant rehabilitated to the best extent possible together with a sum of money or continuing funds to ensure their life-long care and quality of life. There can surely be few jobs as satisfying.

MORE BOOKS BY LAW BRIEF PUBLISHING

A selection of our other titles available now:-

'A Practical Guide to Subtle Brain Injury Claims' by Pankaj Madan
'A Practical Guide to Chronic Pain Claims' by Pankaj Madan
'A Practical Guide to the Independent School Standards – September 2023 Edition' by Sarah McKimm
'A Practical Guide to Estate Administration and Crypto Assets' by Richard Marshall
'A Practical Guide to Managing GDPR Data Subject Access Requests – Second Edition' by Patrick O'Kane
'A Practical Guide to Parental Alienation in Private and Public Law Children Cases' by Sam King QC & Frankie Shama
'Contested Heritage – Removing Art from Land and Historic Buildings' by Richard Harwood QC, Catherine Dobson, David Sawtell
'The Limits of Separate Legal Personality: When Those Running a Company Can Be Held Personally Liable for Losses Caused to Third Parties Outside of the Company' by Dr Mike Wilkinson
'A Practical Guide to Transgender Law' by Robin Moira White & Nicola Newbegin
'A Practical Guide to 'Stranded Spouses' in Family Law' by Mani Singh Basi
'A Practical Guide to Residential Freehold Conveyancing' by Lorraine Richardson
'A Practical Guide to Pensions on Divorce for Lawyers' by Bryan Scant
'A Practical Guide to Challenging Sham Marriage Allegations in Immigration Law' by Priya Solanki
'A Practical Guide to Digital Communications Evidence in Criminal Law' by Sam Willis
'A Practical Guide to Legal Rights in Scotland' by Sarah-Jane Macdonald
'A Practical Guide to New Build Conveyancing' by Paul Sams & Rebecca East
'A Practical Guide to Defending Barristers in Disciplinary Cases' by Marc Beaumont
'A Practical Guide to Inherited Wealth on Divorce' by Hayley Trim

'A Practical Guide to Practice Direction 12J and Domestic Abuse in Private Law Children Proceedings' by Rebecca Cross & Malvika Jaganmohan
'A Practical Guide to Confiscation and Restraint' by Narita Bahra QC, John Carl Townsend, David Winch
'A Practical Guide to the Law of Forests in Scotland' by Philip Buchan
'A Practical Guide to Health and Medical Cases in Immigration Law' by Rebecca Chapman & Miranda Butler
'A Practical Guide to Bad Character Evidence for Criminal Practitioners by Aparna Rao
'A Practical Guide to Extradition Law post-Brexit' by Myles Grandison et al
'A Practical Guide to Hoarding and Mental Health for Housing Lawyers' by Rachel Coyle
'A Practical Guide to Psychiatric Claims in Personal Injury – 2nd Edition' by Liam Ryan
'Stephens on Contractual Indemnities' by Richard Stephens
'A Practical Guide to the EU Succession Regulation' by Richard Frimston
'A Practical Guide to Solicitor and Client Costs – 2nd Edition' by Robin Dunne
'Constructive Dismissal – Practice Pointers and Principles' by Benjimin Burgher
'A Practical Guide to Religion and Belief Discrimination Claims in the Workplace' by Kashif Ali
'A Practical Guide to the Law of Medical Treatment Decisions' by Ben Troke
'Fundamental Dishonesty and QOCS in Personal Injury Proceedings: Law and Practice' by Jake Rowley
'A Practical Guide to the Law in Relation to School Exclusions' by Charlotte Hadfield & Alice de Coverley
'A Practical Guide to Divorce for the Silver Separators' by Karin Walker
'The Right to be Forgotten – The Law and Practical Issues' by Melissa Stock
'A Practical Guide to Planning Law and Rights of Way in National Parks, the Broads and AONBs' by James Maurici QC, James Neill et al
'A Practical Guide to Election Law' by Tom Tabori
'A Practical Guide to the Law in Relation to Surrogacy' by Andrew Powell
'A Practical Guide to Claims Arising from Fatal Accidents – 2nd Edition' by James Patience
'A Practical Guide to the Ownership of Employee Inventions – From Entitlement to Compensation' by James Tumbridge & Ashley Roughton

'A Practical Guide to Asbestos Claims' by Jonathan Owen & Gareth McAloon

'A Practical Guide to Stamp Duty Land Tax in England and Northern Ireland' by Suzanne O'Hara

'A Practical Guide to the Law of Farming Partnerships' by Philip Whitcomb

'Covid-19, Homeworking and the Law – The Essential Guide to Employment and GDPR Issues' by Forbes Solicitors

'Covid-19 and Criminal Law – The Essential Guide' by Ramya Nagesh

'Covid-19 and Family Law in England and Wales – The Essential Guide' by Safda Mahmood

'A Practical Guide to the Law of Unlawful Eviction and Harassment – 2nd Edition' by Stephanie Lovegrove

'Covid-19, Brexit and the Law of Commercial Leases – The Essential Guide' by Mark Shelton

'A Practical Guide to Costs in Personal Injury Claims – 2nd Edition' by Matthew Hoe

'A Practical Guide to the General Data Protection Regulation (GDPR) – 2nd Edition' by Keith Markham

'Ellis on Credit Hire – Sixth Edition' by Aidan Ellis & Tim Kevan

'A Practical Guide to Working with Litigants in Person and McKenzie Friends in Family Cases' by Stuart Barlow

'Protecting Unregistered Brands: A Practical Guide to the Law of Passing Off' by Lorna Brazell

'A Practical Guide to Secondary Liability and Joint Enterprise Post-Jogee' by Joanne Cecil & James Mehigan

'A Practical Guide to the Pre-Action RTA Claims Protocol for Personal Injury Lawyers' by Antonia Ford

'A Practical Guide to Neighbour Disputes and the Law' by Alexander Walsh

'A Practical Guide to Forfeiture of Leases' by Mark Shelton

'A Practical Guide to Coercive Control for Legal Practitioners and Victims' by Rachel Horman

'A Practical Guide to the Law of Driverless Cars – Second Edition' by Alex Glassbrook, Emma Northey & Scarlett Milligan

'A Practical Guide to TOLATA Claims' by Greg Williams

'A Practical Guide to Elderly Law – 2nd Edition' by Justin Patten

'A Practical Guide to Responding to Housing Disrepair and Unfitness Claims' by Iain Wightwick

‘A Practical Guide to the Law of Bullying and Harassment in the Workplace’ by Philip Hyland

‘How to Be a Freelance Solicitor: A Practical Guide to the SRA-Regulated Freelance Solicitor Model’ by Paul Bennett

‘A Practical Guide to Prison Injury Claims’ by Malcolm Johnson

‘A Practical Guide to the Small Claims Track – 2nd Edition’ by Dominic Bright

‘A Practical Guide to Advising Clients at the Police Station’ by Colin Stephen McKeown-Beaumont

‘A Practical Guide to Antisocial Behaviour Injunctions’ by Iain Wightwick

‘Practical Mediation: A Guide for Mediators, Advocates, Advisers, Lawyers, and Students in Civil, Commercial, Business, Property, Workplace, and Employment Cases’ by Jonathan Dingle with John Sephton

‘The Mini-Pupillage Workbook’ by David Boyle

‘A Practical Guide to Crofting Law’ by Brian Inkster

‘A Practical Guide to the Law of Domain Names and Cybersquatting’ by Andrew Clemson

‘A Practical Guide to the Law of Gender Pay Gap Reporting’ by Harini Iyengar

‘NHS Whistleblowing and the Law’ by Joseph England

‘Employment Law and the Gig Economy’ by Nigel Mackay & Annie Powell

‘A Practical Guide to Noise Induced Hearing Loss (NIHL) Claims’ by Andrew Mckie, Ian Skeate, Gareth McAloon

‘An Introduction to Beauty Negligence Claims – A Practical Guide for the Personal Injury Practitioner’ by Greg Almond

‘Intercompany Agreements for Transfer Pricing Compliance’ by Paul Sutton

‘Zen and the Art of Mediation’ by Martin Plowman

‘A Practical Guide to the SRA Principles, Individual and Law Firm Codes of Conduct 2019 – What Every Law Firm Needs to Know’ by Paul Bennett

‘A Practical Guide to Adoption for Family Lawyers’ by Graham Pegg

‘A Practical Guide to Industrial Disease Claims’ by Andrew Mckie & Ian Skeate

‘A Practical Guide to Conducting a Sheriff Court Proof’ by Andrew Stevenson

‘A Practical Guide to Vicarious Liability’ by Mariel Irvine

‘A Practical Guide to Applications for Landlord’s Consent and Variation of Leases’ by Mark Shelton

‘A Practical Guide to Relief from Sanctions Post-Mitchell and Denton’ by Peter Causton

'A Practical Guide to Equity Release for Advisors' by Paul Sams
'A Practical Guide to Financial Services Claims' by Chris Hegarty
'The Law of Houses in Multiple Occupation: A Practical Guide to HMO Proceedings' by Julian Hunt
'Occupiers, Highways and Defective Premises Claims: A Practical Guide Post-Jackson – 2nd Edition' by Andrew Mckie
'A Practical Guide to Financial Ombudsman Service Claims' by Adam Temple & Robert Scrivenor
'A Practical Guide to Running Housing Disrepair and Cavity Wall Claims: 2nd Edition' by Andrew Mckie & Ian Skeate
'A Practical Guide to Holiday Sickness Claims – 2nd Edition' by Andrew Mckie & Ian Skeate
'Arguments and Tactics for Personal Injury and Clinical Negligence Claims' by Dorian Williams
'A Practical Guide to Drone Law' by Rufus Ballaster, Andrew Firman, Eleanor Clot
'A Practical Guide to Compliance for Personal Injury Firms Working With Claims Management Companies' by Paul Bennett
'RTA Allegations of Fraud in a Post-Jackson Era: The Handbook – 2nd Edition' by Andrew Mckie
'RTA Personal Injury Claims: A Practical Guide Post-Jackson' by Andrew Mckie
'On Experts: CPR35 for Lawyers and Experts' by David Boyle
'An Introduction to Personal Injury Law' by David Boyle

These books and more are available to order online direct from the publisher at www.lawbriefpublishing.com, where you can also read free sample chapters. For any queries, contact us on 0844 587 2383 or mail@lawbriefpublishing.com.

Our books are also usually in stock at www.amazon.co.uk with free next day delivery for Prime members, and at good legal bookshops such as Wildy & Sons.

We are regularly launching new books in our series of practical day-to-day practitioners' guides. Visit our website and join our free newsletter to be kept informed and to receive special offers, free chapters, etc.

You can also follow us on Twitter at www.twitter.com/lawbriefpub.

www.ingramcontent.com/pod-product-compliance
Lightning Source LLC
LaVergne TN
LVHW022053200926
848481LV00003B/890
9781912687015